CW01498237

Mark Palmer is a professionally q and change practitioner. He is facilitated brand and change con Executive Head of Strategy and Communication Planning at some of the world's most regarded advertising agencies. He was named the strategist in *Campaign* magazine's fantasy agency of the millennium. Mark has been part of the teams who've launched, positioned, repositioned and sustained some of the world's most famous and notable brands, including BMW, Pepsi, Orange, Google, Sony, Channel 4, *The Economist,* Cadbury, Bupa and more. Mark has helped position numerous start-ups that have gone on to grow successfully and be sold. He's helped many of these brands rethink their approach to marketing and communication, from product placement to pop-up shops to brand partnerships. Mark guest lectures at the Henley Business School, the School of Communication Arts, and previously at the Copenhagen Business School. He runs the branding and marketing module at the London Business School Launchpad programme, where start-ups look to develop their business and seek investment to launch.

Praise for *The Work Smarter Guide to Marketing*

'In today's marketing environment, we all need to have our BS card ready, and Mark has written a crisp, compelling guide to help us all be mindful of what matters and not to get distracted by what doesn't. A very enjoyable and informative read.'
David Wheldon OBE, Former Global Head of Brand at Coca-Cola, Vodafone and Royal Bank of Scotland.
President of World Federation of Advertisers and host of the
***Better Marketing* Podcast**

'Mark Palmer treats marketing the way a physicist treats the universe: with curiosity, clarity and the courage to simplify. Someone whose advice has never let me down.'
Jamie Milroy, CEO and Founder of Dash Rides

'Whether you are on the board of a company, running your own business, have a side-hustle or have found yourself in a job in advertising, sales or marketing...READ THIS BOOK. You'll find your fear of marketing and its bullshit falls away in front of your eyes.'
Lisa Batty, Global Comms Planning Director of TikTok for Business

'This book drop-kicks the bullsh*t out of branding. It's not another soft-focus LinkedIn sermon about "authenticity" – it's a marketing defibrillator. Palmer doesn't whisper sweet nothings about purpose; he rips the mask off and shows you the wiring.'
Mark Borkowski, Founder of Borkowski and author of *Improperganda: The Art of the Publicity Stunt* and *The Fame Formula*

'Actionable frameworks, readily understandable examples and clear writing – with just the right touch of humour. This is a book for marketeers to keep close at hand!'
Claire Hewitt, Director of The Henley Partnership, Henley Business School

'In a world where everything is changing, we need to listen to Mark Palmer, who understands what doesn't change about marketing better than anyone.'
Richard Hartell, CEO of EssenceMediacom USA

'I've known and worked with Mark Palmer in multiple companies. It's about bloody time he wrote a book. He thinks differently and connects dots you didn't even see. Most of all, he has always made marketing seem so very obvious and easy, when many are befuddled by it. Grab this book – it will save you thousands of hours of angst, shedloads of wasted money and help make you look like a genius.'
Ali Crossley, Managing Director, Distribution, Legal & General

'Most people in marketing don't understand marketing. That's the uncomfortable truth Mark Palmer sets out to fix – with clarity, humour and real-world wisdom. At the School of Communication Arts, we train the most awarded creatives in the world. I always want them to meet Mark, because he doesn't just teach marketing – he makes them think.'
Marc Lewis, Dean of the School of Communication Arts

THE
WORK SMARTER
GUIDE TO
MARKETING

Better Marketing Without the Bullsh*t

Mark Palmer

Series Editor David Kean

ROBINSON

First published in Great Britain in 2025 by
Robinson

10 9 8 7 6 5 4 3 2 1

A CIP catalogue record for this book
is available from the British Library.

ISBN: 978-1-40878-315-3

Typeset in Sentinel and Scala Sans
by Ian Hughes

Printed and bound in Great Britain
by Clays Ltd, Elcograf S.p.A.

Papers used by Robinson are from well-
managed forests and other responsible
sources.

MIX
Paper | Supporting
responsible forestry
FSC® C104740

Robinson
An imprint of
Little, Brown Book Group
Carmelite House
50 Victoria Embankment
London EC4Y 0DZ

The authorised representative
in the EEA is
Hachette Ireland
8 Castlecourt Centre, Dublin 15, D15 YF6A,
Ireland
(email: info@hbgi.ie)

An Hachette UK Company

www.hachette.co.uk
www.littlebrown.co.uk

To Team Palmer. To Siobhan, who I should have got to write this book more intelligently and more beautifully. To Hector, who would promote it better than me and invest any money made more wisely. To Matilda, who would have got this book out way earlier, keenly spotted any mistakes sooner and still joyfully taken the pi**. To Ralph, my little new business buddy, whose calming pats of his tummy and woofs to 'Be More Ralph' inspired for so many years.

Contents

Introduction

Simple can be harder than complex: you have to work hard to get your thinking clean to make it simple. But it's worth it in the end because once you get there, you can move mountains.
STEVE JOBS, INTERVIEW WITH *BUSINESS WEEK*, 1998

Marketing is important. Research conducted among more than 200 financial analysts who cover publicly listed companies in the United States and United Kingdom revealed that 'strength of brand/marketing' is the factor most frequently cited by financial analysts (79 per cent) when asked how they appraise the companies they cover. This was ahead of leadership quality (76 per cent) and technological innovation (72 per cent).[1]

But something's up in the world of marketing. It's become too complicated and confusing. Most marketers know this. A common understanding of what marketing means is being torn apart on all sorts of false dichotomies – like you need to choose to spend on brand vs performance. It isn't either/or.

In a world where marketing has become cluttered with complex jargon, endless acronyms and marketers run after the latest, 'shiny' trend, this book offers a refreshing return to the essentials:

- Putting yourself in the mind of your customers.
- Designing products and services with benefits that meet their wants, needs and desires.
- Differentiating meaningfully from your competitors.
- Finding ways to attract your customers' attention so they buy you, your products and services.

What's happened?

Imagine having a medical procedure or walking over a bridge knowing there is a 50 per cent chance that the surgeon operating on you or the engineer who built the bridge wasn't qualified. How comfortable would you feel going into surgery or stepping across a bridge over a ravine? Yet, according to the publication *Marketing Week,* more than half of all marketers surveyed (53.8 per cent) say they have not studied a marketing-related academic or professional qualification of any kind.[2]

There is an unbelievable level of marketing misinformation, conflation of terms and *supposed* expert bullsh*t in circulation. As marketing has added more tools and complexity, many people with the word 'marketing' in their job title have roles where they focus only on specific specialisms within marketing – e.g., advertising or sales. Advertising and sales are *part* of marketing, but they are not marketing. Marketing is much less potent when this role confusion occurs and business suffers as a result. Marketing has also become a soup of acronyms – B2B, B2C, B2B2C, AI, CMS, CPC, CRM, CTA, CTV, NPS, PPC, ROI, SEO, UX. It's a real mess. (If you want to know what all of these mean, there's a glossary on p. 137.) Now with over 1 billion members, what is shared in posts on LinkedIn compounds the confusion and misinformation. Dr Chris Arnold, Founder of Creative Orchestra, described LinkedIn as 'a place where everyone is an expert even when they aren't'. That's certainly true for marketing.

Having deep expertise in a specialist marketing area can often make it harder to be open-minded when your market or customer changes. For example, if you are a specialist in digital marketing or a content creator, you are vulnerable to a concept known as the 'law of instrument' (or Maslow's Hammer). Whatever the problem is, you view it only through your specialist lens. The same way that if your only tool is a hammer, you tend to see every problem as a nail.

The marketing world we live in may be complex, but that doesn't mean we must make it even more complicated.

If you asked someone in the street which brand's marketing they liked, they might say Apple's or Nike's. Certainly, these companies' marketing has been very effective: Apple is the world's most valuable brand, worth well over $1 trillion.

Both Apple and Nike spend huge amounts of money on marketing in all kinds of ways. They create a space for their brand in people's heads. Doing this positively affects the decisions people make in their brand's favour. Millions of people make a choice, pay a premium, and remain exceptionally loyal to these brands as a consequence. This is what smart marketers do. If you want the technical term, it's called brand *saliency* – making sure your brand comes to mind in buying situations.

Apple and Nike did good marketing from the start. In the case of Nike, Phil Knight, a college graduate, and his former track coach, Bill Bowerman, created a better running shoe to get better traction for athletes on race tracks (product); they priced it just below the premium brands like Adidas, offering quality and value (price); sold their shoes out of the back of their cars near track meets (place); and sold them personally (promotion) to persuade runners to buy.

See. It doesn't have to be complicated.

Marketing applies to whatever industry you are in. It matters to people personally when they're looking for a new job or when companies want to attract talent. The question of 'Why should we hire you?' or 'Why should you join us?' needs a marketing answer. Marketing is needed to sell products and services, to persuade people to donate to charities, give blood, not to drink and drive, and to get people to vote for a political candidate.

When researching this book, I spoke to several leading marketers and successful branding and advertising agency leaders who have helped businesses build marketing success. One of those was Marc Nohr, who has guided some of the biggest brands in the world, including Amazon, Carlsberg, Hilton, Lexus, Starbucks and UNICEF.

Marc has presented to many boards that viewed marketing with cynicism. If you've worked in marketing, it's likely you will have heard someone senior in a company say they are not affected by marketing or advertising. Many people genuinely believe they are impervious to it. I asked Marc how he answered this. He said he asks them what they have bought recently and why. Whether it was a car, a meal in a restaurant, a movie, make-up, a plumber or a mobile phone, he asked them to talk through the process leading up to the purchase and then he'd ask: 'So, why did you finally choose X, Y or Z?' Marc was reminding these people to think like *customers* again – with needs and choices in a competitive world – so they realised how marketing affected them really.

You may have picked this book up because you are beginning a start-up business, run a business-to-business firm, are working in one aspect of marketing now and want to expand your horizons or are just curious to understand what this thing called 'marketing' is. Whoever you are, my starting point for advice is to put yourself in *your audience's mind*. Focus on three things.

1. Understand your audience/customers' *wants, desires and needs.*
2. Work out how your brand is beneficial and different from alternative brand choices (or better than doing nothing at all).
3. Find a way to connect points 1 and 2 to make customers more likely to buy or do something in your favour.

Things go wrong when companies forget this simple start point. In the last few years, Nike has been among those brands that have lost their way. When writing this book, its market capitalisation was still valued at $71.6 billion. However, its valuation fell nearly 5 per cent in a year. That marked the second year in a row of a decline. Sales continued slipping.

In September 2024, after five years at the helm, Nike's CEO, John Donohoe, an ex-management consultant and technology business leader, resigned. He was replaced by Elliott Hill, a former sports trainer and Nike 'lifer'. Nike's share price immediately increased by almost 10 per cent.

It's harsh to blame Nike's problems on one person, especially one who managed them through COVID-19. Yet Nike is a compelling case study of how easily a brand can get the basics of its marketing wrong.

Nike became overcomplicated and riddled with corporate jargon. Advertising investment was called 'demand creation expense'. When they admitted they had spent too much on performance marketing and not enough on brand marketing, Nike said they 'over-rotated the shift to digital'. Nike wanted to change how people bought shoes – forcing customers to buy online instead of making their shoes available to try in real-life shops. Instead of being about the audience's passion and interest around sport, Nike focused on age and gender. Almost as an epitaph to what Nike got wrong, Bloomberg published a feature story on Donohoe before he departed titled 'The man who made Nike uncool'.[3]

This Work Smarter Guide is designed for anyone who wants to give their business the edge that great marketing can create, but who are intimidated by the preponderance of jargon or frustrated by marketing's current state.

This book will pull the curtain back on some of the simple genius in the marketing moves of some iconic historic brand stories. It will make marketing tangible using a variety of real examples of when marketing gets it right and when it gets it wrong. It will walk you through approaches you can apply. It will share some of the key questions to ask and answer to be a better marketer without the bullsh*t.

I hope you'll enjoy reading the book. It sets out to return to doing simpler (and, therefore, better) marketing and to be accessible and useful. I want to provide an antidote to the prevalent marketing bullsh*t. Think of it as a handy marketing 'recipe' book that will help you create marketing which has a better chance of working – a distillation of the best insights from seasoned experts, real-world examples and proven principles to help you make smarter marketing decisions.

1

What Marketing Is and What it Isn't

The great enemy of communication, we find, is the illusion of it.
WILLIAM H WHYTE, AUTHOR AND JOURNALIST,
FORTUNE MAGAZINE, 1950

The word for cat in Italian is 'gatto'. The word for cake in French is 'gateau'. They may be spelled differently but they sound the same. I've always had this vision of someone getting a 'birthday cat'. Regarding what marketing is and its terminology, we see birthday cats all the time.

Marketing would love to be science or a profession, like medicine or the law, with agreed definitions, rules and procedures. But marketing is neither of these things and it has got into a muddle as a result. There isn't one instruction manual for marketing.

Asking Google 'What is the definition of marketing?' doesn't help either. One highly read article resolves the issue by listing seventy-six different expert definitions! So, I'll come off the fence and pick some examples of what better marketing is and what it isn't – and explain why. My choices are based on what has worked and been helpful when working with company boards, start-up founders and practising marketers in the real world.

Better marketing is based on the specific business or challenge you face

It's always dependent on the situation facing the brand, the market, the challenge and the audience. Seth Godin, one of the most influential writers about marketing, has a definition of marketing that's worth sharing: 'Marketing is the generous act of helping someone solve a problem. Their problem. Marketing helps others become who they seek to become'.[4] (I'd add: 'and do what they want or need to do'.)

Key to doing better marketing is to put yourself into the mindset of your audience and to see the challenge from their perspective – not yours.

Any customer is either on a journey, or needs to be encouraged to start one

Better marketing assists a customer on their journey, so they end up choosing you as their destination and doing something about it.

Better marketing is the process of asking better questions about your audience's journey and then figuring out better answers to those questions.

Get the answers to these questions wrong and you'll end up as the marketing equivalent of the failed explorer, Captain Scott. He talked a good game and spent a fortune but didn't think ahead: he didn't ask or answer the most critical questions. Consequently, he and his doomed team never made it back from the South Pole and were beaten by the better-prepared Roald Amundsen – an explorer who asked better questions and had better answers. (Ironically, Captain Scott does have residual brand awareness but as an example of heroic failure.)

When you look at brands and marketing that have been successful, you'll find they asked and answered better questions on behalf of their audience. Here's an example of what I'm talking about.

CASE STUDY: MOVEMBER

Early detection of prostate cancer in men can make the difference between life and death. Back in 2003 there were three issues stopping early diagnosis.

1. Men were not aware, or discounted the symptoms, of prostate cancer.

2.   They were reluctant to discuss it openly.

3.   They put off getting tested because they didn't think it would happen to them.

The Movember campaign team put themselves inside their audience's heads. They asked why these problems existed in men's behaviour and how they could change them. They started with thirty men in Australia rethinking the problem. They thought from the perspective of how they could leverage the way men behave in their favour.

At the time, charity marketing focused simply on raising awareness and asking for donations. It would establish those most likely to donate and the most cost-efficient way to reach them – money out to get donations in. Movember changed this. They didn't adhere to the playbook for charity marketing. They turned charity from an individual request for funding into a collective challenge for 'Mo Bros' to take part in.

Moustaches were out of fashion at the time. So, the challenge became to grow a moustache to raise money and awareness for prostate cancer in the month of November. They got men to reach out to their friends and families to sponsor them for a fun activity on a serious issue. In the process this raised awareness, destigmatised the issue and created a database to communicate with year after year. Movember expanded beyond Australia. As social media grew, so did Movember. Today, they've extended the men's health issues they tackle from prostate health to men's suicide – and many other issues in between.

Since 2003, Movember has raised $911 million and funded more than 1,250 initiatives globally. Their work has led to a number of positive outcomes. For example, Movember's annual 'Know Thy Nuts' campaign (aiming to raise awareness of testicular cancer and how to check for it) reached 20.4 million people globally in 2013 with 4.1 million completing a video on self-checking.

Better marketing is where science meets art

My next definition is from Dr Philip Kotler, often referred to as the father of marketing and author of eighty books on the subject, including *The Principles of Marketing*. Dr Philip Kotler defines marketing as: 'The science and art of exploring, creating, and delivering value to satisfy the needs of a target market at a profit. Marketing identifies unfulfilled needs and desires. It defines, measures and quantifies the size of the identified market and the profit potential.'[5]

Now let's apply this definition to Movember. Kotler believes marketing is both a science and an art. There was hard data on the difficulty of changing men's attitudes and behaviours. The art was to rethink how men could be engaged, the creativity of the name and the iconic moustache branding.

For Kotler, marketing is exploring. It's a skill applied to a situation for an audience, not an instruction manual. There were known rules to how you marketed for a charity – Movember reinvented them. Marketing is dynamic; it explores and creates. Movember started in Australia, and was originally focused on prostate cancer. The event itself remains in November. But in terms of where it does what it does, how it does it and the marketing methods it uses, it refreshes them every year.

In terms of Kotler's definition that marketing is a pursuit to define an audience's unmet needs and desires, Movember couldn't be clearer on this. It's men's ignorance of prostate cancer and helping them get out of their own way to prevent them dying early!

Finally, Kotler states that, when done well, marketing creates a value exchange for what the business offers against its audience's unmet needs. Movember demonstrates this – it has dramatically raised awareness of prostate cancer. Today, men and the media openly discuss prostate cancer and what to do about it. Men are more willing to get proactively tested. And the men who have taken part in Movember enjoy it and feel proud of what they've helped achieve.

Better marketing is about knowing what you stand for and making choices

When customers are given too many choices, they freeze. People have a fear of making the wrong choice. If you offer them too many options or things to consider it may trigger them to find additional options. Next time you go into a major retailer, notice how they leave space between the entrance and promoting any offers. They don't want to scare you off with too many choices before you're properly in the store. Marketing is about making your customers' decisions less, not more, complicated.

Given that Steve Jobs created the most valuable brand in the world, I should share his definition of marketing and say why it's worth paying attention to: 'Marketing is about values. It's a complicated and noisy world, and we're not going to get a second chance to get people to remember much about us. No company is. So, we must be clear about what we want them to know about us.'

Marketing is a game of 'consumers catching' – not a game of 'businesses throwing'. If you throw too much, your audience won't catch anything. And they are more likely to catch things from organisations whose values they believe and trust.

Whilst in some instances people will research a purchase in depth (e.g., a mortgage), in most cases, our personal beliefs and values drive many of our daily decisions. Even when choosing between two mortgage products at the same rate, you are more likely to buy from the company you know and trust. Values are a main factor in a purchase decision. Values also affect the ability of a company to attract and retain staff. In a study by Qualtrics, employees who say their company's mission, vision and values align with their own are far more likely to recommend their employer as a great place to work (70 per cent vs 25 per cent).[6]

Now think of a brand you have bought recently or might buy in the future. You won't have a long list of things it does in your head. You'll have a mixture of images, ideas, associations – ideally, they'll all reinforce each other. (What comes to mind if I ask you about Apple, KitKat, Guinness or Tesla?)

Better marketing is about building a relationship with your audience beyond what they buy

Forget what you think you may have learned about marketing in *The Apprentice* TV show. Each week, both the US and UK versions of *The Apprentice* pit teams against each other to solve what are often marketing challenges. For example, the contestants create new products – but without ever talking to their audience or researching their market! Typically, as the deadline looms to meet the sales target, they cut prices and sell to *anyone*. In order to maximise profit (and so beat their competitors in this task), the truth is bent in their sales pitch or they don't deliver what they promised their client. Nobody in *The Apprentice* has to go back in to get people to buy that product again next week or next year. The people in next week's task don't get to meet last week's customers.

This leads me to the definition of marketing from Steve Dawson, President of Walkers Shortbread: 'Marketing is products that don't come back and consumers that do.'

Hype or hyperbole are tempting ways to sell a product. Yet, when the customer reality kicks in it leads to brand disappointment. This is corrosive to trust. It reduces confidence to buy again or recommend to others. If you believe marketing is spinning a yarn to make one transaction and disappearing before you get found out, you aren't a marketer, you are a grifter. Apple didn't become the world's most valuable brand because its customers bought an iPhone once.

Having explained some key views of what marketing is, I'll now share my views on what marketing *isn't*.

Marketing is NOT sales. Marketing is NOT advertising

I think it's important to address these two common misconceptions about marketing.

Both sales and advertising are part of marketing. In fact, they are a subset of one of the 4Ps – promotion (see Chapter 5, p. 48). They are a vital part of creating outstanding marketing.

Marketing, advertising and sales are all on the same side. They work best when working together on a shared mission. Too many marketers pass the baton to sales to make things happen, rather than seeking their insight and ideas on how marketing can improve what can be offered and communicated. The danger is that when marketing is seen as synonymous with sales or advertising, we miss the bigger opportunities for insight, ideas and more powerful joined-up solutions marketing should bring.

For example, before 2014, if a bank customer lost their credit or debit card, they had a simple choice: cancel their card with the bank or run the risk that it might turn up but might also have been stolen by someone who would use it, landing you with the bill for their purchases. It took a 2014 start-up, Metro Bank, to introduce the concept of 'freezing' your card. This is a great example of unmet customer needs being identified, leading to a product innovation which could then be advertised and sold.

Marketing and sales share the goal of attracting prospects and converting them into profitable customers. In the division of labour and roles, marketing should be more focused on understanding the customer and the market, and on helping create products and services the customer values. And then finding ways to effectively communicate and engage with customers so they become interested and more likely to buy. All at a profit.

Sales work directly with prospects or distribution channels to gain a presence and reinforce the value of the company's solution in order to convert prospects into customers.

To use an analogy I read from an American marketer, a marketer's job is to lob the ball to the batter (sales). While the batter (sales) smashes it out of the park; without the marketer, sales don't get off the ground. Without the sales representative, the ball is dropped. Marketers set the stage for salespeople to walk on and get an ovation from the audience.

Great salespeople can sell ice cream to Inuits. Great marketers mean they don't have to.

The tools to do marketing may have changed. Customer journeys may have changed. However, what marketing is about fundamentally hasn't changed

The confusion in what marketing is and is not has become more exaggerated in the digital age.

Nike, whom we mentioned in the introduction, is just one example of how marketing has been hijacked to mean something much narrower. Nike's marketing was (and still should be) about identifying an audience with an unmet need, finding a way to solve that need and then delivering and communicating the solution. It did this year after year. But the customer journey changed, as did the tools. How Nike did marketing also changed.

Nike fell into the trap of bottom-up marketing – letting marketing be defined by digital and data use. This led to an over-reliance on immediate returns and an obsession with visible metrics. It became focused on performance marketing (driving sales) at the cost of joined-up total marketing that included brand building. It was investing in serving and retaining demand – not on *creating demand* to start with. Innovation suffered and talented staff members left.

When marketing is only (data) science, the art disappears. When everyone learns and applies the same best practice tactics, how do you stand out except by spending more or cutting your prices and margins?

Of course, any smart modern marketer today would see optimising digital, data or using AI as hugely important. Many businesses and brands are created, defined and built on this – businesses such as Uber, Airbnb, Just Eat, Meta, Salesforce, Adobe and many more. But none of these businesses define what marketing is from the 'bottom up'. As you read these companies' names, notice how images and associations immediately arrive inside your head. There's much more going on beyond just the data.

Better marketing looks to find out what really happened when using digital and data

There has never been more 'rich' data, where a customer profile can include purchase history, demographics, website browsing behaviour, social media interactions, customer support interactions and more. It can be found and used at a faster speed. It can then be analysed, tested and applied in real time. This should all be part of gaining more insight into the market, the consumer and into the world they live in today. There have never been more ways (or channels) to do marketing. But beware of being distracted by the digital and data sugar high.

Imagine you created a new restaurant, and you wanted to attract customers. You could use Instagram, get dining influencers to recommend it on social media, get it reviewed in the evening paper, put local leaflets through people's doors, put it up on posters at the nearby train station. You could buy geo-targeted ads on people's mobiles when they move about in your area in real time. You could buy your restaurant name and 'restaurants in my area' as search terms on Google.

Imagine you did well and you got bookings at the restaurant. Some bookings came via the website, some called to book, some just walked in, some came via OpenTable. Of course, as you are investing money in these channels you would want to optimise that spending against where the customers are coming from. If you've tracked it properly, you'll have lots of data on views and clicks on all the digital channels. But what data do you have about the posters, the press ads, the restaurant review? About the word of mouth from those who visited?

Because you have digital and data supposedly linked to bookings, you'll be tempted to use it. After all, you can see things such as who went from search to your website. But what if they went to search after seeing the poster or seeing the review? Unless you've thought ahead to find out how you might evaluate what might be the cause and effect (e.g., asking those who booked to respond to a survey), you'll never know. If you haven't thought to ask for their contact details, you won't have started building a database with which you might email them in the future to come again, or ask them to recommend you on Tripadvisor.

Now, if you think this scenario describes what marketing is, you need to think again. You're in danger of falling into the trap that the success of your restaurant's marketing is defined by the return on advertising and use of media, including digital and data.

You must remember, no matter how good the media or digital or use of data was, it's not what matters most in marketing. If you have yet to figure out a coherent and distinctive offering for what your restaurant is all about or got the product, price, promotion and place right, you will ultimately fail. People may come once, but why would they come again or recommend your restaurant to others?

However, if you've created a great restaurant brand idea that your desired customers love and you've applied the best digital and data marketing as part of your approach, then WOW!

It isn't the other way round.

Marketing people must understand their 'sales funnel' (how they functionally progress to turn visitors into leads and leads into customers) or their customers' journey (a more detailed map from the customer's perspective that shows how people go from just hearing about a product to actually buying it) including digital and data. Better marketing is about keeping an open mind and looking to evaluate the bigger picture of how a decision is affected from the customer's perspective. This is something Nike forgot. Many marketers do.

Marketing isn't about expecting data to give you the answers to the marketing challenges you face. Marketing is about utilising data about consumers and their behaviour in a market alongside human imagination to create insights that help inspire ideas that then deliver actions.

2

Who, Why, What and Where is Your Audience?

Your audience gives you everything you need. They tell you. There is no director who can direct you like an audience.
FANNY BRICE, ACTRESS[7]

At the heart of marketing lies the audience. When thinking about the audience, try to avoid being transactional. Most marketers and businesses approach their audience as if it's a static group. Every audience is a mosaic of overlapping identities, needs and desires. Looking at them through just one lens – e.g., age or income – limits your ability to understand what drives them. Great marketers use multiple lenses to view who their audience might be. And they apply what they learn from using multiple lenses laterally. They design products or services with their audience in mind. They don't see their audience as a target to hit; rather, they see them as someone to reach, connect and engage with. They think who, why, what, where:

Who: Identify the audience you are trying to reach.

Why: Understand their motivations and behaviours.

What: Focus on what you will do to craft a compelling offer or communication.

Where: Decide the best way to deliver the offering or linked message through the right channels.

EXAMPLE: MARKETING A NEW FITNESS APP THAT GIVES FIFTEEN-MINUTE WORKOUTS

Traditional audience lens: Target young professionals aged twenty-five to thirty-five in urban areas.

Marketing idea: Instagram ads showing busy workers squeezing workouts into a hectic day.

Different lenses: Define your audience based on their aspirations and the barriers that get in the way of doing a workout.

- **Lifestyle:** Busy parents looking for efficient workouts.
- **Marketing idea:** Create content about short workouts while kids nap.
- **Behaviour:** Fitness beginners are intimidated by gyms.
- **Marketing idea:** Develop ads featuring 'judgement-free' home workouts.

Let's focus on busy parents as a potential audience for the fifteen-minute fitness app.

Who: Working parents with young children trying to juggle everything in an endless work–life balance.

Why: They envy other parents who seem to stay fit and have it all. They'd like to get healthier and avoid developing a dad or mum bod as they age. They've tried gyms and other things. They want quick, effective workouts to fit into their busy schedules.

What: A fitness app syncing to your watch or phone that notices your behaviour. It will politely nudge you when you could be getting fit rather than scrolling on TikTok. It will monitor and analyse areas of behaviour linked to movement, sleep and mobile phone usage. It will prescribe and offer fifteen-minute solutions delivered by video or audio or with the option of real-time coaching.

Where: Instagram, TikTok and YouTube are places where people seek fitness advice. They are also places to interrupt wasted time that fitness could replace. School groups and community or interest areas might reach busy parents of young children. Put a stand at a farmers' market or school fairs. Posters near walking paths or family exercise meet-ups. Buy ads for the audience next to digital audiences looking to book a holiday (the known frustration of wishing you looked fitter on holiday). Partner with a family holiday company and do a shared offer to their database. Create research on how parents who are the 'taxi service' to take kids to activities but don't feel fit themselves. Share in PR and go on Breakfast TV, Mumsnet, etc.

Ten audience lenses to try (there are more)

1. **Demographics:** Age, gender, income, education, ethnicity, marital status and occupation (e.g., marketing luxury items to high-income professionals aged thirty to forty-five).

2. **Psychographics:** Psychological attributes, including values, beliefs, interests, attitudes and motivations (e.g., eco-friendly products to sustainability advocates).

3. **Behaviours:** Buying habits, brand loyalty, frequency of use and preferred purchasing channels (e.g., loyalty programmes that offer the existing member a discount if they bring a friend).

4. **Hobbies and interests:** Activities and passions that engage your audience's time and attention such as sports, arts, gaming, reading, travel (e.g., partner with relevant associations or influencers that align with these interests).

5. **Lifestyle:** A person's way of living – daily routines, consumption

patterns, work–life balance and social habits (e.g., offer products or services that seamlessly fit into your audience's daily lives).

6. **Geographic factors:** Where your audience is located – urban or rural, regional differences, climate differences, travel patterns (e.g., campaigns to align with local preferences or regional events).

7. **Cultural and social influences**: The shared norms, values and practices of a group – traditions, religious beliefs and social roles (e.g., a campaign that uses the ritual of the football fan and their hopes for their team at the start of every season).

8. **Contextual:** Situations where they may encounter your product or message at a time or place that may trigger relevant associations (e.g., at work, during their commute or while relaxing at home, at the airport, as couples at the cinema).

9. **Purchase intention:** Internet and other shopping behaviours – are they actively shopping, passively browsing or unaware of their need (e.g., tailor your messaging based on where they are in the decision-making process)?

10. **Media consumption and influence:** What media, platforms, apps and channels do they use to gather information or entertain themselves? Whom do they trust or are influenced by in social media (e.g., media partnerships, brand partnerships, influencer activity)?

How to discover your audience

There have never been more ways to discover your audience. In our digital age many of these are free.

Go into the real world of your audience

It's terrifying how many marketers never go and meet their customers, experience their audience's journey, listen in to customer service calls or go through the experience their target audience gets with a competitor. Data can be misleading. It will tell you what is happening in sales, but not why.

Customer interviews. Engage with customers directly through interviews or focus groups – find out in depth how they discover your brand, navigate the market, their decision-making process and other influences.

Research surveys and questionnaires. I'd advocate professional help on this if you can afford it. It helps to know how to ask questions and interpret data without bias. If you have a database, you can contact your customers to get their opinion. You can use several questionnaires and analysis tools like Survey Monkey to gather direct insights from potential or existing customers.

Social media analytics. Platforms like Meta, X and TikTok offer both creator tools and audience insights. You can cross reference interests in an area, e.g., fitness video watching with demographics or engagement data. All these platforms also offer a search function as a user. This can be flipped so you search words or interest areas to see what content is being consumed and is popular with an audience.

Website, app and search analytics. It's absurd to have a website, an app or a digital path to your brand without analysing it. Analysis reveals the behaviours of your audience, their reaction to your offering, your messaging and their journey to you. In a business of any size, you should have professional skills. For smaller firms, fear not, there is a wealth of free analytics and plugins like Google Analytics or Google Keyword Planner that show search trends that can indicate what your audience is interested in.

Market research reports. If you are interested in an industry or an area, someone is likely to have written a report on it. Seek out industry reports from sources like Statista, Nielsen or Pew Research Center for high-level trends and benchmarks. Companies will create their own research for marketing purposes. You can often get a free PDF of a report in exchange for your email address.

Industry associations, events and groups. These provide great opportunities to understand and meet people in an industry and get their in-market perspective. Research papers and audience insights are frequently shared.

Competitor analysis. You are not the only one trying to figure out your audience. Investigate what your competitors are doing and see if you can gauge their level of audience understanding and try to identify gaps in it which you can fill.

Forums and communities. Monitor Reddit, Quora and LinkedIn discussions or niche-specific forums to understand audience needs and opinions. Ask questions in the forums.

CRM and sales data. Leverage your own data from CRM (customer relationship management) systems. This used to be the domain of big companies. Now, capabilities like HubSpot or Salesforce can help identify patterns and audience understanding available in customer data to the smaller business.

Stay open and lateral when using audience data. You can do this by:

- **Asking different questions**. Don't just look to find the answer to 'Who is my audience?', but also to 'What drives their decisions?' and 'What barriers might prevent them from engaging with the brand?'

- **Mapping their world.** Create detailed profiles and personas for your audience, integrating different lenses. Use that persona to rethink how you might reach them or message them.

- **Experimenting.** Test your audience hypothesis and the messages you think will motivate them. You can go back into focus groups and ask your audience to react to your brand idea and messaging. You can message audiences with ads or offers with control tests and use what is known as A/B testing to see what resonates.

- **Staying curious.** Stay fluid in how you see your audience over time. Technologies, social norms and other trends change. Ensure your audience understanding is up to date. New entrants arrive and existing audiences leave. Make sure you are best placed to do something when that happens.

Selecting channels where you can best reach your audience. Find where the focus of your audience and the different channels you can use overlap. Start by fishing where the fish (your audience) are most likely to be. Think:

- **Omnichannel location:** Store, app, digital, event, email, etc.
- **Media location:** Within digital (sites or audiences), search (keywords), broadcast (channels, shows, buying audience), billboards, cinema, newspapers/magazines, inserts/leaflets.
- **Physical location:** Geography, context, e.g., airports for travel.
- **Timing:** When are they most active and receptive, e.g., New Year's resolution for a fitness app.

Pilot, measure, test and learn. Get into the real world with real audiences and experiment. Get feedback and learn from people trying products. Mystery shop, run test markets or control cells with media to find out whether your media channels are working to improve brand and sales.

3

Insights, Ideas, Actions

Strategy without tactics is the slowest route to victory. Tactics without strategy is the noise before defeat.
SUN TZU, CHINESE MILITARY STRATEGIST, *THE ART OF WAR*

I'm about to say something that will get me shot by many people with marketing in their job title. It's bullsh*t to say data is the answer.

Data can take many forms. A marketer must always remember that it is just data. Data alone is not an insight. Data does not do your thinking for you. It's how we use the data that reveals an insight we can act on.

Whether you have vast amounts of data available in real time as a business or are working out your side hustle in your bedroom, the power of your data or research doesn't lie in having it. It lies in how effectively you can transform it through three strategic behaviours. Each plays a vital role in transforming information into meaningful outcomes that affect your audience to the benefit of your brand.

1. Insights
2. Ideas
3. Actions

Marketing is about problem-solving for humans – especially humans in businesses. It requires logic but it also requires critical understanding, imagination and action. As the momentum of AI always being the answer takes hold in business and in marketing, we must not lose sight of these two realities:

- We are marketing to humans.
- Humans can do things that AI doesn't do, e.g., we can apply critical thinking and have imagination. Humans can see things that aren't there and solve problems with limited data.

The role humans play in solving problems

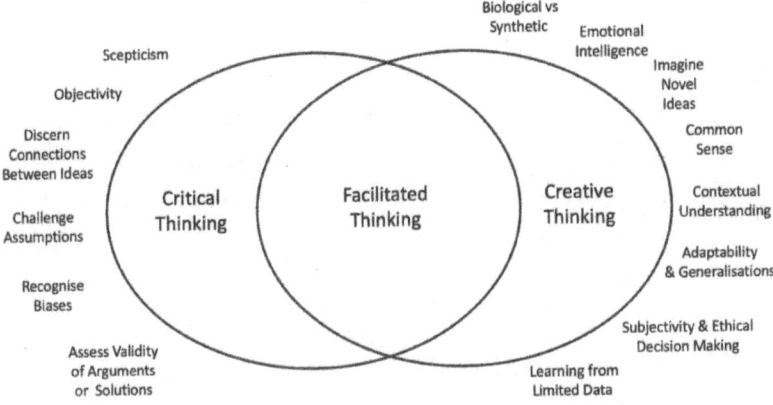

Whole rafts of new products, services and businesses have evolved from data and digital in the form of mobile, the cloud and connected devices. However, the marketing benefits are not the data. It is us – human beings – who turn data into insights, ideas and actions that solve problems in people's lives and that's what brings brands to life. It is this that may be assisted by AI.

Take, for example, satellite navigation systems. GPS data spawned the rise of sat navs. Initially leading the way were TomTom and Garmin, both of which produced sat navs for cars. TomTom saw GPS data as a way to compete in the car sat nav market. Another, Garmin, took the same GPS data and it became an insight that led to an idea to develop new products in new markets to create new behaviours to track, monitor and motivate human fitness and sport. Active people who play sports benefit from being able to track and motivate themselves to keep fit using devices which monitor their performance over time. TomTom has a market cap of $650 million. Garmin has a market cap of $41 billion (larger than Ford).

CityMapper is an app that connects data from various transport options on your mobile in real time. The benefit is it allows you to discover alternative journey plans. It will string together many connection paths across transport, including when transport is due to arrive or leave, to give you choices and options for travelling from A to B.

If you buy car insurance, an insurance aggregator brand (like Go.Compare in the UK) lets you enter your insurance data and needs. It then matches that data to car insurers' policy data. The benefit for insurance companies is a market of potential leads without having to spend much on advertising. The benefit for consumers is not spending hours calling companies or filling in forms to get the best offer. It helps you get the job done in seconds.

Uber takes traffic, driver and passenger journey data and calculates a solution presented to your phone at a price in real time. Passengers benefit from getting from A to B with just a few taps of their mobile faster and cheaper than the alternative of contacting taxi companies directly or hailing a cab on the street.

What is an insight?

An insight is a moment of clarity when an underlying truth reveals itself that explains why people do what they do. Insight is the foundation of a brand's strategy. It tends to uncover something new about who they are, why they behave the way they do, what motivates them or what they need. An insight is the foundational truth that unlocks understanding about your audience, market or challenge.

An insight is typically:

- A deeper understanding of the emotions, needs or motivations of your audience.
- A different perspective that reveals new opportunities or challenges.

- A fascinating fact, a unique piece of knowledge that guides strategy and might spark creativity.
- Something that you didn't know before.
- Something that may change the way you think about the problem.
- The 'why' behind the 'what'.

An insight isn't:

- A data point or statistic in isolation. For example, knowing 'Gen Z consumes twice as much video content as Millennials' is just a piece of information, not an insight.
- An observation without context. For example, 'People would like all travel to be hassle-free'. It lacks specifics and depth. Observing an event with data – for example, '40 per cent of our cosmetics users prefer hand creams' – is also a data point, not an insight.

Five steps to find your insight

1. Explore context. Capture and note down the context from the consumer's perspective by explaining the background in a straightforward way. What are your observations of how your audience behaves in a market situation? What does your audience currently think and feel? Put yourself in their shoes to consider what they want to achieve and why.

2. Identify their dilemma. Consciously or unconsciously, an audience is making choices and what influences their choices may not be easy to see. Be open-minded about what a dilemma might be. It might be attitudinal, behavioural, desires, wants or needs. Don't be rational; look for emotions. The 'This Girl Can' campaign changed attitudes and behaviour to women's fitness. The facts were, 75 per cent of women said they wanted to do more sport. However, the dilemma holding them back was discovered to be the 'fear of being judged' for their appearance, their performance and their priorities. Ask yourself what barriers you need to be aware of that stop your audience from doing what they want with a product or service.

3. What's their why? Try to figure out why your audience behaves the way they do. If you are to develop a brand offer, product or service, it must be able to boost or change this behaviour.

4. Expose their drivers. The frustration that stopped women taking up sport was the fear of being judged. The opposite are the drivers. In the case of 'This Girl Can' this was that the support and desire for female camaraderie can be used to prompt an action. So, find frustrations and then figure out the drivers. What unfulfilled needs are they trying to satisfy? What tensions are they trying to resolve? Are they frustrated with how the market operates or how they experience the product? Think laterally: is there something in their head, heart, society or their relationships?

5. Imagine nirvana. What is their perfect world, and how would they think and feel if we made it happen? You are still doing insight, so don't skip ahead to ideas and actions. Think about how they'd like to feel as a customer.

Once you've found your insight, it is likely to help you answer some key questions. Consider what this data/research reveals about customer behaviour, needs or motivations that:

- Surprises or makes you think.
- Could open doors to better connect your brand and its marketing to your audience's needs or issues.

Let's look at some real-world examples that show how insights are essential to successful marketing.

Dove's 'Real Beauty' campaign is a well-known example of

uncovering an insight into mainstream women's cosmetics. The insight was that most advertising for cosmetic products glamorises women and is narrow in its representation of them. Many women felt under-represented and uncomfortable in their own bodies because of it. This truth created a foundation from which Dove could engage in a new conversation with women about what beauty really means.

Florida was a pivotal state to swing when Barack Obama ran for President of the USA in 2000. However, there was a lot of misinformation claiming Obama was not American and was of Muslim origin. Florida had a large older Jewish community whose votes were vital to Obama's prospects. It wasn't proving easy to get them to listen to his policies. The insight was that the people most likely to persuade older Jewish people to listen to what Obama stood for were their grandchildren. Younger Jewish people throughout the USA were very pro-Obama. A campaign called the Great Schlep was conceived. This was built from a website and tools to help young Jewish Obama voters contact their grandparents with talking points by email, phone or visit and then encourage them to vote for Obama.

Insights come from having curiosity. Robin Wight, Chair at the advertising agency WCRS which was responsible for BMW UK's 'ultimate driving machine' brand work, described his role as *interrogating the product until it confesses its strength*. His team would routinely meet the engineers and designers at BMW in Germany rather than just take briefs from the marketing team in the UK.

What is an idea?

An idea is the spark of creativity, innovation or change. In marketing terms, it is not just advertising or creative materials; it can be a whole set of thoughts about what the brand can do across all the 4Ps or what might be a fifth P in partnerships. (See Chapters 5 and 6.) An idea could also be a product innovation, a new distribution strategy, a new way of working, a partnership or a loyalty programme. What matters is that it *directly addresses the insight* in a meaningful and creative way.

Fundamentally, an idea is an imaginative concept that brings your insight to life. An idea connects your understanding of the audience with a compelling way to engage them.

An idea typically:

• Is a clear, actionable, creative or strategic concept that responds to the insight.
• Acts as the bridge between understanding the customer and uniquely addressing their needs.
• Makes what the brand stands for resonate with the audience meaningfully.

An idea isn't:

• A wish or a dream.
• A generic, random or disconnected execution or marketing concept.
• A campaign that ignores insights in favour of getting on topical trend bandwagons.
• Running a promotion to give a new beer away at half price without a deeper connection to your audience or brand is not an idea. It's a tactic.

Let's revisit the Dove 'real beauty' campaign to see how they went from insight to idea. Their insight showed that women often feel unrepresented by traditional beauty standards. The idea was to challenge this perception head-on by running a campaign for Dove which showcased real women of all shapes, sizes, ages and ethnicities. Dove wanted to create an open debate, raising questions for other brands and the cosmetics industry. At the same time, they wanted to resonate emotionally with all women and get them to reciprocate with the brand.

On a visit to BMW engineers in Germany, the advertising agency learned that every aspect of a BMW was designed to make the car perfectly balanced. This attention to detail meant putting heavier things like batteries in the boot/trunk. They also learned that to make a convertible safe, the car could take the weight of another BMW convertible on the roof. The idea was to explore ways that showed the cars' strengths using 'torture tests' in extreme conditions (see actions, p. 32).

What is an action?

An action is the tangible thing you do to make your ideas real. It's the execution of your strategy and ideas. This can take many forms in marketing, depending on the brand's goals and values. Actions need to be joined up and true. You can't say you are the best for customer service and not deliver it. You can't say you are bothered about the environment in your charity partnership and be caught having a supply chain that isn't. You can't say you are exclusive and yet be available everywhere.

An action typically:

- Is purposeful and aligned with the brand, strategy and idea.
- Has measurable steps to bring the insights and ideas to life.
- Follows through into joined-up tactics. How will it work across digital marketing, influencer partnerships, experiential events and product innovations?

What an action isn't:

- Repeating or mimicking something the competition does.
- Disconnected marketing activities that don't align with insights or ideas.
- Marketing activity and campaigns without clear metrics for success.
- Actions that don't lead to meaningful engagement or brand loyalty.

Take a look at these examples of brands that took action after coming up with ideas inspired by insights they uncovered.

For BMW, the advertising agency dramatised balance, strength and safety using a 'torture test' which showed one BMW convertible perfectly balanced on top of the windscreen of another convertible – without the top on either of them.

Coca-Cola had an insight that it could increase the idea of buying and sharing with others if it made the design of a Coke more personal. The action became the 'Share a Coke' campaign. In this, Coke changed the labels on its bottles, replacing the logo with popular first names of people. The product became both more personal and more interactive, with people looking out for their or friends' names and sharing. It also reconnected the brand to moments of shared happiness.

Spotify has the insight that music is like the heartbeat or mood map of people's lives. The idea was to take the data on music from all its listeners and for you, the individual listener. At the end of every year, Spotify now releases Wrapped, which it offers to its users for free. You can see your music behaviour trends and influences. It's a celebration of the fans, artists and creators who made a year of listening, showing users how their taste in music evolved. Spotify Wrapped has become an individual user and highly publicised brand media event.

Joining up insight, idea and action: First Direct

First Direct was a pioneer in digital banking in the UK. Whereas most digital banks focus on tech as the driver to solutions, First Direct, as a brand, always focuses on understanding what customers really value.

Their insight

By leveraging customer feedback and market research, they recognised the growing frustration with impersonal service and inconvenient banking hours. First Direct was configured to deliver the opposite: simplicity, 24/7 accessibility and personalised service.

Their bridge from insight to idea

This insight led them to look for an idea to position themselves as a modern alternative to traditional banks.

Their idea

First Direct's idea was to be the 'unexpectedly human bank' in a digital-first world. Many banks were transitioning to online services to reduce their own costs. First Direct retained the human touch in customer interactions. It offered a blend of technology and personalised customer service. They emphasised qualities like friendliness, availability and trust.

Their action

- **Exceptional customer service:** Their teams are available twenty-four/seven. There is no reliance on automated phone systems for initial interactions. Customers are immediately connected to a human representative. They reset the standards for the industry.
- **Simplified digital experience:** They invested in user-friendly apps and online platforms. The user experience was one of the first to ensure customers had easy access to banking services without feeling overwhelmed by complex systems.
- **Empowered customers:** They offer financial tools, advice and personalised solutions that align with their customers' life goals.
- **Transparency and trust:** They communicate clearly and straightforwardly in their policies. They build customer loyalty and confidence in their brand. In the most recently published UK Customer Satisfaction Index, First Direct is the most highly rated organisation for customer satisfaction – across all sectors and industries.

4

What is a Brand?

It takes twenty years to build a reputation and five minutes to ruin
it. If you think about that, you'll do things differently.
WARREN BUFFETT, AMERICAN INVESTOR AND PHILANTHROPIST,
IN ONE OF HIS BIENNIAL LETTERS TO BERKSHIRE HATHAWAY
MANAGERS IN 2014

Would your brand or business pass the dinner party test?

David Wheldon OBE is one of the world's most renowned brand builders. He oversaw global brands such as Coca-Cola and Vodafone. He helped turn Vodafone into the UK's most valuable brand. Following the 2008 financial crisis, he was at Barclays and then RBS (Royal Bank of Scotland), unpicking the damage done to their brands, businesses and the UK by banks.

I saw David address a room of cynical city traders at Barclays. This was when Barclays was at the lowest point in the bank's – and banking's – reputation. He was challenged to explain why fixing the Barclays brand mattered. He explained it was easiest to do it backwards. He asked the traders to think two to three years ahead and imagine going out to dinner with people they didn't know. 'When those people ask who you work for and what you do, if we get the brand right, you'll feel much happier to admit you work at Barclays. And you'll be able to explain why.'

When I asked David to give me a definition of what a brand is and how you would measure it, he gave me two quotations:

'A brand is what a brand does.' Arun Sarin, Former Global CEO Vodafone.

'A brand is what people say when you are not in the room.' Jeff Bezos, Amazon.

Sarin means that a brand is the sum of everything it does – much more than just the ads, logo and brand colours. For example: when writing this chapter, a huge media storm had just broken out about changes Jaguar were making to its 'brand'. The entire row was sparked by a teaser commercial and changes to its logo – nothing more. This was before Jaguar had even launched a new car. This furore epitomised all the confusion of 'expert' commentators and consumers around the subject of brands. Nobody had seen the car yet, yet the media and supposed experts were all totally sure they understood the new Jaguar brand.

Tesla doesn't really make ads – but it's a brand. Gore-Tex is a technology and also a brand. Its brand sits inside other brands. Salesforce is a brand. Switzerland is a country, and it has a brand. Donald Trump has a brand.

Jeff Bezos' quote tells us that a brand is the perception of your audience, suppliers, agents, partners – it's what they'll actually say about your brand (which you might not want to hear). One way of measuring this is called the Net Promoter Score (NPS). According to *Fortune* magazine, this is used by two-thirds of *Fortune 1000* companies to measure customer satisfaction.[8] The question NPS asks is: 'On a scale of 1-10, how likely are you to recommend business XYZ to a friend or family member?'

You'll never be great at marketing if you don't understand what a brand is.

Why strong brands and good marketing matter

At a basic level, a brand allows you to be differentiated, legally protected and charge more than your competition. The concept of a brand (or 'mark') can be traced to different places and times. For my American friends who think it comes from the Wild West and branding cattle, I'm sorry to disappoint you. The Egyptians did that around 2,700 BCE (Before Common Era).

The original reason for branding was to mark one's property for ownership. Depending on who the brand was owned by, it conveyed a level of quality. This extended to owning brands as trademarks. Coca-Cola, for example, would use its trademark so it could show its brand was distinctive. Buyers were willing to pay a premium compared to a large number of other colas that existed because they knew they were getting 'the real thing'.

Why build a brand today?

- A brand gives a product or service a distinct identity in the mind of the consumer and the market.
- It helps the audience discover, remember and create associations with the benefits the brand brings and the value that they gain as a result.
- It lifts and separates the product or service from the competition in the mind of the audience and other partners within the market.
- It provides trust and reassurance when people buy and use it.
- It allows a premium to be charged over competitive alternatives.
- It can provide a cost-effective way to launch or build other associated products under one brand name, e.g., there is the Apple brand and the sub-brand iPhone.
- It can provide defence for the business against new entrants or market change. Stronger and more established brands are more likely to stay in a purchase repertoire. Coca-Cola began in 1886.
- It can add significant value to the business beyond sales and profits.
  - It can increase the share price or the value of the company when sold.
  - It can help to develop partnerships and relationships with other brands.

Brands have a value on the balance sheet and are viewed as an intangible asset – major international brands such as McDonald's, Coca-Cola and Disney represent, by some estimates, 50 per cent of their company's value. Nike's share price went up by 9 per cent and Starbuck's up by around 20 per cent when their CEOs left. Among the reasons was that market analysts believed the brands were in better hands under the new CEOs, who both had strong records for brand understanding and brand building.

What is good brand marketing?

- Good brand marketing keeps a company's brand front and centre in people's minds, especially at the moment of decision-making. It thinks and acts from a '360-degree perspective' on what a brand is, what it does and how it behaves.
- It always puts itself in the mind of its audience and how they view the brand, their decision process and competitors.
- It understands the difference between articulating the brand's image, look and messaging, and joins up the *entire* brand experience: product, display, customer support and service, purchasing experience, user experience, delivery, after-care, etc.
- It understands that it is the guardian of the brand from the past and its custodian for the future. Brands can be updated and sometimes repositioned, but brands should be wary of changing without a very good reason.

Let's play brand poker

Defining, deciding and delivering what matters most for a brand will always be specific to your audience and your market. Stop for a moment and do the exercise below.

Think of seven factors that help a consumer make brand comparisons when choosing a vacuum cleaner:

1 _____

2 _____

3 _____

4 _____

5 _____

6 _____

7 _____

Within that list, pick the three that are most important.

Now, imagine you are actually looking to buy that product. You only have a choice between a vacuum from Dyson or Bosch. Which would you choose and why?

This is how brands work. As the customer you perceive things from inside your own head. You give, often subconsciously, different attributes you perceive matter varying degrees of importance. Then, you weigh up in your mind how well a brand matches your wants, needs or desires.

Most of the time, a brand is typically looking to do four things:

- Beat the competition to make itself the preferred choice against the factors that matter.
- Not slip up on a factor that could lead you to reject it, e.g., it is not good value for money, has a reputation for breaking, is dated, or can't be trusted.
- Alter or affect perceptions of shared values so that the customer will have a greater affinity with their brand now and in the future.

- Look to secure the highest margin from the customer for the product/service sold – without being perceived to take advantage.

In the simple scenario above, Dyson may leverage the inventor and engineer credentials of their founder. (They dramatise that by showing the product's internal workings.) The core values they want to share might be innovation and design. They may play up their British heritage. None of which means that suction power or impartial reviews in the purchase process don't matter. It's just where they focus to build clear associations in your mind.

Bosch might build their brand difference from their power tool roots. They may focus on its power, robustness and durability to differentiate the brand. They may play on its German heritage and that country's association with engineering excellence and efficiency.

From a customer perspective, both companies have now played their brand hand. Like betting on their best five cards in poker. But unlike poker, where there is a strict set of rules on what makes the winning hand, in *brand* poker what makes for a winning hand is inside the customer's head.

At some point in this scenario both Dyson and Bosch may review and research how their brand is doing. Will they need to adapt to become the preferred choice against each other in a future game of brand poker?

- Dyson may discover their design is working really well, but Bosch is known for being more powerful.
- They might discover that media coverage about Dyson moving manufacturing overseas has tainted the positive associations it has with being British.
- They might discover Bosch is doing really well with younger renters in their first flat and that power is becoming a bigger factor in purchasing decisions for all sorts of products, including women's hair dryers. Dyson might think the brand needs to offer

new products and increase its power story to boost its appeal to younger people.

- Alternatively, Dyson may decide not to jettison their brand strength in design and innovation. Instead, they may need to find a way to build on those strengths even more. They might also see some research saying that noise is becoming a key issue in people's lives – and so ask their design team to create a powerful vacuum that is also quieter.

- Bosch may discover they're known as the most powerful vacuum but lose on design associations. They may do something radical and get a famous car designer to work on a new product.

- Bosch also read the research on the concerns about noise, so put in place an internal review of all their products – not just vacuums. If noise is a major issue for Bosch's audience in the future, then to protect the brand they need to do something about it now.

So many choices to make. Here's the stripped-down version of what building a brand is about in five key points.

1. Understanding your audience's needs and motivations *from their perspective*.
2. Creating and communicating things across *all* aspects of your brand (product, price, promotion, place and possibly . . . partnerships) that differentiate you in a meaningful way from the competition.
3. Living the attitudes, values and behaviours the audience believe about and experience with your brand – which gives them added confidence and trust in your brand.
4. Not standing still in how you deliver what your brand stands for or re-imagining it.
5. Articulating, creating and communicating this in a joined-up way

– not only in its product, price, promotion, place and partnerships, but in the logo, advertising, strapline, packaging, events, behaviours, etc.

The content for those five things will differ by brand, market and audience. What a women's fashion brand needs to think and do is different from a car insurer or a fitness centre or accounting software for a small business.

A step-by-step process to build your own brand

As I have said, all brand building is specific. However, there are some key steps to follow. (See also the Brand Key process as a worked approach in Chapter 12, p. 126.)

1. Understand and review your core mission and values

This is the foundation of any brand. Ask: why does this organisation exist? (See Chapter 7, p. 72, and Chapter 8, p. 82.)

2. Understand your audience

A successful brand speaks directly to its audience's needs, beliefs and aspirations. Research is normally critical to identify and understand the audience you want to reach (see Chapter 2, p. 17).

3. Conduct competitive analysis

The picture your audience has of the market and your brand will be affected by what your competitors do. Investigate and understand their marketing and current brand positionings.

4. Create a distinctive visual, sonic or behavioural identity

It's only at this stage that you look at a brand's visual elements – logo, colour palette, typography and imagery. These must be distinctive and aligned with the core values.

5. Build a consistent brand experience, voice and messaging

Brands need consistency in tone of voice, messaging and language to build trust and recognition. Your brand's voice should reflect its personality and values. Ensure all people in the organisation understand the brand and stay 'on brand'.

6. Convert the brand into joined-up behaviour and communication

Turn the brand mission and its goals into relatable, emotional ideas and narratives. Perceptions that Nike is superior to other sports shoes is because of the story that the brand has told us for years around its athletes.

7. Engage through meaningful campaigns

Now that you have a brand, how are you going to turn it into marketing campaigns and activity?

8. Measure, monitor and evolve

Brands must evolve based on audience feedback and changing contexts. Measuring the brand performance from the audience's perspective ensures ongoing alignment with goals and helps identify areas for improvement.

Your brand isn't what you put down on paper – it's what exists inside your audience's head

When I asked Marc Nohr what a brand was, he described it as 'The space you occupy inside your audience's head'. Your brand doesn't exist on charts or in a PowerPoint deck. It exists in the perceptions and actions of your audience. What you let out of the door for the brand – be it a product, social media post, customer service response – isn't necessarily in your control. Out there in the real world, all sorts of people attach all sorts of meanings to words. So, what you mean may not necessarily be what people see, hear or believe. People make up their own 'magpie's nest' of associations – what counts is not the message you transmit but what message people receive. These are not the same thing.

Always remember that:

- Your brand is not what you put in. It's what your audience perceives it to be.
- Consumers react and create associations with a brand *emotionally*, in pictures, sounds, colours, stories, smells. The children's brand Play-Doh has patented its smell because it is emotive of the brand.
- A consumer's reality is the sum of all aspects of the brand they experience. Virgin Media can have hugely creative TV advertising for its broadband speed in the UK, but it's also the most complained-about company for customer service. When Virgin Media is 'not in the room' nearly 100,000 people give it an average score of 1.4 out of 5 on Trustpilot, the customer review site.
- If your brand is fake on the inside, expect it to come out in public. Sadly, examples of this abound, but two have recently become infamous: the Post Office in the UK and Boeing in the USA.
- Your competitors, media and social media influencers have their own brands to push. They'll translate what you say from *their* perspective – not yours.

The audience will mainly think about your brand as a mixture of associations, experiences, prejudices, images, sounds and more. The marketer's job is to organise, integrate and articulate the brand experience so it has the most positive outcome for the brand and the customer. Which is why brand building is an art, not a science.

Just think about yourself: day after day you play this game

without even thinking about it. You are not thinking, 'Why did I decide to get a McDonald's instead of a KFC?', or 'Why did I choose to order it on Uber Eats rather than Just Eat?'

When you come to make a purchase decision you may research it, ask others for their opinion, check out reviews, do a price comparison against alternatives. You might believe you are making a rational choice. You are not. Harvard Business School Professor Gerald Zaltman estimates that 95 per cent of decision making occurs subconsciously.

If you bought car insurance recently, you might tell yourself that it is a very rational purchase. But you probably bought it through a price comparison site – why did you go to that one instead of any of the many others? When it came to your final insurance choice and you didn't take the cheapest, did you really rationally analyse what it was about the company you ultimately bought from that made you choose them?

Brand building: what you can learn from Guinness

If you are brutal about Guinness, it's just a stout. As a stout, it's black and white. Being black and white as a stout is not unusual. You could drink Murphy's. It's black with a white head too. Guinness is also a drink. You could go into a pub and order a lager or a bitter. We all know Guinness comes from Ireland. We all know Pimm's is English. But Guinness is known, drunk and distributed around the world. Pimm's, however, still has 70 per cent of its sales in the UK and mainly in the south and in the summer.

Guinness is a masterclass in how great brand building looks easy, but there is genius in how the brand is built, thinks and behaves. Below is an example for Guinness that I borrowed and adapted from Walter Lim of Cooler Insights, one of Singapore's most renowned business bloggers.

Let's call this the Guinness brand onion. No consumer would recollect all the elements if asked. However, Guinness adds layer upon layer of different aspects to its brand story to make the whole greater than the sum of the parts. So, the brand perceptions of Guinness are multilayered, interconnected, emotional, rational, textual, etc. At the centre, which everything builds out from, is the brand promise. Building out at the next layer is its personality and the facts and symbols that it connects to make its brand more tangible, but also differentiated. Then on the outside layer Guinness connects to consumer needs and desires in how they'd describe it, how it makes them look, how it makes them feel and what it does for them.

It is worth noticing the consistency of the Guinness brand. This doesn't mean it stands still. There is always ongoing brand innovation. If you've been to Dublin, you may have done a tour of the Guinness Storehouse and the Gravity Bar (opened in 2000). Most recently it launched Guinness 0.0 (its alcohol-free version), which is soaring in sales and distribution. It caters to changes in social and drinking behaviours. The way Guinness 0.0 has been developed, from taste to positioning to communication, is to reinforce not dilute the overall Guinness brand. In the UK, Guinness is not just the number one stout, it is now the number one selling beer. It's also fundamental to 'brand Ireland'.

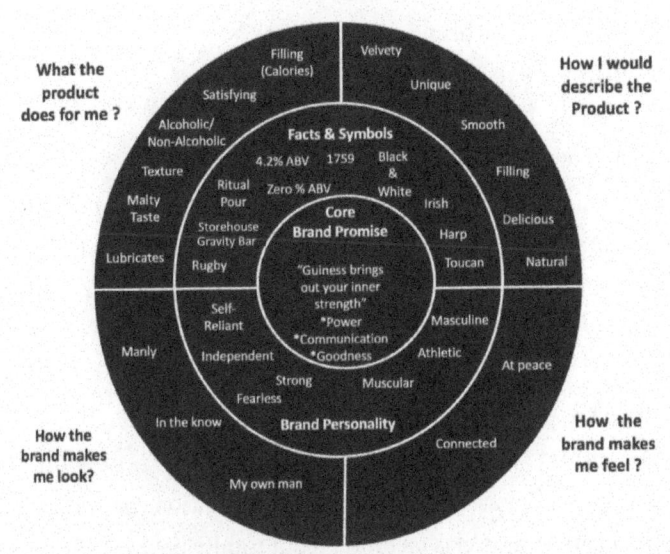

Here are the key lessons from Guinness that are worth applying when you look to develop a brand:

- Draw your brand associations or create a mood board of them. Use words, stories, images, sounds, history. Put these on the board. Move things around until you're happy with it.
- Don't just make it about the functional delivery of a product. Make it emotional. Know and tap into your brand mission, values and personality.
- Think of and use different senses. Guinness is obviously a physical product you consume, but it has texture, a slow pour, the black and white imagery, associations (St Patrick's Day, rugby, etc).
- Root it all around the perceptions of the audience. What benefits does your brand bring and what quantifiable value does it give to your audience's lives? Guinness asks four questions on this brand 'compass'.
  - What does the product do for me?
  - How would I describe the product?
  - How does the brand make me look?
  - How does the brand make me feel?

What do you want your customers' answers to be?
- Have a limited number of fixed brand cues and symbols that you consistently use and reinforce. For Guinness, it includes black and white, the pint symbol, the harp, the slow pour, the Irish heritage, dancing man music.

What would be yours?
- Keep brand consistency when innovating with new products, new ways of marketing, new brand associations or channels.
What could you do that was *on brand* – but totally new?

Check your brand bank account – paying into and borrowing from the brand bank

If there are fault lines between what a brand claims and the lived reality of its customers, those fault lines will eventually be exposed – with all the ensuing carnage that this entails. Sadly, there are many large corporations who convey one thing in their communication while doing the exact opposite to their customers in reality. For example, the UK payment protection insurance mis-selling scandal took years to come out. Banks had been misleading customers while claiming to be on their customers' side. By 2021, these banks had paid out £38bn in compensation.

Robin Wight describes how brands are like aeroplanes: 'They take a lot of fuel to take off. Once in the air, you can fly them on less fuel. You can even turn the fuel off, and they'll glide briefly. However, if you leave it too long, they stall. No matter how much fuel you now put in or how hard you pull on the joystick, it's too late, and it crashes.'

Building a great brand requires investment financially, in human resources, energy and the diligence to keep sight of what your brand is about. Brands don't just need builders, they need guardians and they need champions. It isn't one person or just the marketing department, it's *everyone* in the organisation understanding the brand and driving it in the same direction.

5

Understanding the 4Ps of your Marketing Mix

The whole is greater than the sum of its parts.
ARISTOTLE, GREEK PHILOSOPHER

The American academic, Neil Borden, suggested that marketers see themselves as chefs mixing ingredients to create a better meal. He came up with the idea of the 'marketing mix'.

E. Jerome McCarthy took it one stage further and suggested marketers think about the 4Ps of marketing – product, price, place (distribution) and promotion. He saw these as the most common variables used to construct a marketing mix. From these 4Ps you could craft a marketing strategy and a plan.

The 4Ps have changed over time – people keep adding new ones, merging existing ones and inventing new models. Some of the Ps overlap – they always have. Go back to the idea of cooking. We now have many different types of food and new ways to cook, buy, deliver, experience and store. But a cookbook with some essential recipes is still handy.

This basic marketing cookbook uses the 4Ps. They are useful, easy to learn and apply. They help you think about what you need to do in your total marketing mix. They give you four key factors which must be thought through and executed smartly in order to market a product or service successfully.

Product

This is the good or service being marketed, sold or made available to your audience. It could be:

- Something physical (a can of beans)
- A service (a ride from A to B on Uber)
- An experience (a concert, football match, gym workout)
- A promise (we'll pay your insurance claim if your car is stolen)
- An action or behaviour (don't drink and drive)
- A location to meet and share or buy things (Facebook, X, Etsy)
- Somewhere to find and discover things (Google, Chat GPT, price comparison websites)
- Scarcity (Ticketmaster)
- An ingredient brand others buy and use to show quality (e.g. Gore-Tex, Dolby or Carl Zeiss lenses (from glasses to mobile phones)
- A badge or standard – Kitemark, Michelin stars.

Ideally, your product or service should fulfil an existing consumer demand or unmet need. What your product or service offers determines how much to charge, where to place it and how to promote it. (That's the other three Ps.)

Price

Price represents the amount charged to customers for a product or service. It directly impacts sales volume, revenue and profitability. In setting a price, consider both internal costs and external demand to create value for customers while supporting a sustainable business model. Look at your competitors' prices and consider how you compare. Look at your price from the bottom up (your costs plus a fair margin) and from the top down (what the market and your audience will pay).

Pricing can be structured as a one-time payment, a subscription or a 'freemium' model (where basic services are free, but additional features are paid).

In B2B, tech companies often use a SaaS model (software as a service). For example, Salesforce charges businesses on a per-user, per-licence basis. This approach is ideal for selling to large companies with many users, as the incremental cost of adding more users is low. Also, the more integral Salesforce becomes to a company's operations, the harder it is to switch to another platform.

Some companies, like Ring, use variable pricing:

- Buy the product and install it yourself.
- Buy the product with installation included.
- Buy the product and add a subscription for video monitoring.

Your decisions around product, price, place and promotion are interconnected.

Some businesses are the gateway to supply and demand in a market. This allows them to offer bid pricing where customers bid up against each other to secure something. For example, art auctioneers or how keywords are sold in search results on Google.

Markets with limited availability and time-sensitive demand allow for 'dynamic pricing'. This is where algorithms calculate the price charged based on changes in demand – think airline seats, concert tickets and Uber. Many businesses, especially online or mobile, use algorithms and AI to predict and price via forecasting supply and demand. They have access to large amounts of data on customers, the prices people buy at, website demand and other linked traffic or data. For example, the announcement of European Champions League football fixtures increases demand for flights to cities where the teams will play. These joined-up data-led businesses can optimise decisions concerning the best price *and* the deployment of the product or service – e.g., Uber car availability near me and the price. Hotel apps may have a higher price on a mobile search if you are in the area (they know you need a hotel more urgently). People know to search in incognito mode on Google or via a virtual private network (VPN) so that previous searches for flights don't push up the price on a repeat search.

Dynamic *monopoly* pricing seeks to extract as much as possible from the customer. This can lead to prices at many multiples of the original price. For example, ticket prices for the Oasis reunion concert via Ticketmaster saw fans not only queue for hours, but as they got to check-out they saw the prices change, adding hundreds of pounds per ticket. This exploited both the greater demand, but also the fan fears they would not get back in the queue if they refused to pay. This caused a backlash from fans and can be seen as profiteering, which adversely affects brand perceptions. Ticketmaster is being looked into in the UK under consumer protection rules, and its holding company, Live Nation, was taken to court by the US Department of Justice in 2024.[9]

Online ordering portals, such as Just Eat and Uber Eats, can charge anywhere from 15–35 per cent commission on every order they process from the takeaway restaurant. As there are now multiple takeaway apps, the restaurant owners weigh up the different benefits and costs of being on these apps or not.

When buying from a wine list, people will often make *relative* price decisions. They don't buy the most expensive or cheapest bottle, but something in the middle. The consumer doesn't necessarily think about whether the price for the wine chosen is a good absolute value. Similarly, airlines offer Premium Economy. Customers pay more money for a minor upgrade to an economy seat. An inverse is to keep the prices more stable but increase profit margins by what is known as 'shrinkflation'. The price stays the same over time, but the size of the portion goes down. Chocolate bars and sweet tins were bigger in the past.

It's important to remember that the right price drives the right amount of sales and profit. The price must be related to the product/ service's value to the buyer – whether perceived or actual.

When calculating the profit return of pricing decisions, it's essential to consider whether the pricing decisions made might also lead customers to move back or forward a purchase and change the 'whole life value' of a customer for the business. A retail shop may offer 50 per cent off to boost sales, but it needs to factor into the final profit calculation any discount offered. Attracting people using the discount may just pull forward sales that would have happened anyway later at full price – thus cannibalising your profits. And poor pricing may lead to a reluctant purchase and lost repeat purchases due to a loss in future loyalty. Overcharging for a restaurant meal may mean customers never come back. Undercharging, or being too cheap, may cost your business credibility, which is why some advisory businesses, for example, and luxury items set a high price to be 'reassuringly expensive'.

Another growing area is conditional pricing. Pricing may be free or higher *on condition*. For example, Spotify, Amazon and Netflix all offer cheaper or free subscriptions if you accept advertising. An ad-free service costs more.

In conclusion, a well-thought-out pricing strategy balances profitability, customer satisfaction and brand positioning within a competitive marketplace.

Place

This is where the product is sold and how it's distributed to customers. At its most simple for consumer products, this means a physical retail store or an e-commerce website. It may also be via a reseller and a supply chain. You may go into a wholesaler or have an agent (think house buying) who is part of your distribution chain. You may sell via a market or a platform.

Place should consider your customers' behaviour and purchase journey. Ice-cream vans are positioned in places where kids go on sunny days for a reason. If you are selling airline tickets to Champions League host cities, paying for search ads next to fixture searches would be smart. If you are a pharmacy, you may want to be on the list available for prescription fulfilment at doctors' surgeries.

Purchase journeys often include visits to major online retailers and resellers such as Amazon and CompareTheMarket. These are places too (even though, if you pay for them, they're also a promotion).

Place will include what page matters most to land on on a website, or what aisle or shelf a product should be on in a store. My publisher might ask what it's worth for this book to be in the bookstore window versus just on a shelf?

Depending on your industry, there may be key shows or events you need to be seen at, high-profile guides that customers read and review sites for service ranking. In a world of social media and content creators, having your own presence like a shop or stand may also be a key place decision. Offering an app is a crucial place decision.

If you need to attract the right talent for your business or be located where all the industry talent is already working – think Silicon Valley for tech talent – then place is a key decision.

Usually, the ultimate goal of 'place' is to determine the best way to get products in front of the customers who are most likely to purchase them.

When buying, customers will also operate across multiple places in the physical and online world. They may research in a shop but buy cheaper elsewhere online. This is called 'showrooming'. You need to connect the places you are considering with your customers' potential purchase journey.

This type of consumer behaviour means that businesses need to consider their 'omnichannel' policy. And to look not just at the return on investment by channel but at the totality of the return across all channels. For example, Nike's decision not to be in general sports retail shops yielded higher initial margins, but meant they started to disappear in purchase journeys which began with general sports shopping in stores. It also ultimately pushed Nike's prices down on its online retail as a way to attract sales. Theatrical releases of movies in cinemas rarely cover costs but they do affect perceptions and generate reviews which can lead to greater overall returns for a film over time – when they get streamed or from associated merchandise.

Places (and purchase journeys) will reconfigure by market as society changes and your competitors change their behaviour. For example, AA Cars (Automobile Association) states 48 per cent of motorists in the UK had bought new cars without visiting dealerships. Following massive behaviour changes due to the pandemic, by 2022 Just Eat had 18 million customers. Being on such apps is a key place decision for takeaway businesses. It never used to be.

Market models of place can also completely change over time. The rise of streamers like Netflix, Amazon, Disney and Discovery has completely changed the distribution and revenue models for TV shows, films, documentaries, sports and advertising. It affects the audience of ad-funded businesses on ITV and Channel 4 in the UK and NBC in the USA. It's affected the subscription model for Sky Movies, Sky Sports in Europe and ESPN in the USA. We used to own music on vinyl or on CDs but now more people subscribe to Spotify to listen to it (though vinyl has increased recently – partly because it gives something tangible to own as a memory of a favourite artist or concert).

Place and promotion are tied closely together: you can actively hijack customer journeys to change or bring forward decisions. If an online retailer is worried that a customer may be browsing but not about to buy, they might push a promotional message: 'last hotel room available' or 'try free now, unsubscribe later'. Conversely, a retailer with a website and stores might offer faster delivery if you click and collect (as this will take you into a store where you may buy more).

Promotion

The last of the 4Ps of marketing is promotion. A helpful way of thinking about promotion is to break it into paid, owned or earned.

- **Paid**: It costs you to get your product or service promoted. It wouldn't appear unless you paid someone to do it for you. Advertising and having a salesforce are classic examples.
- **Owned**: Where you've created and own your own content. For example a website, event, database to promote to where you might send a weekly newsletter, a shop where you can control the experience.
- **Earned**: Doing things to appear in media, editorial or references/reviews without appearing to pay for it. It may take significant work to achieve this, such as winning an award, a review calling your product the 'best hair dryer', or a five-star restaurant rating. Often, it will include paying for PR (public relations) to ensure your actions and news get into the media and achieve exposure in the most positive way.

Promotion includes all the advertising and public relations that make up your promotional strategy for your product. It includes discount offers, BOGOFs (buy one get one free) and free trials (check how many online subscriptions you still have – and pay for – because you forgot to cancel them after the free trial expired).

Promotion includes sales. That means salespeople and how they sell – which may well be supported by the other Ps. It includes having demonstrators to teach consumers how to use a product.

Online marketing is a massive area for any business these days. How you configure your website or app and tag it matters – doing this is called search engine optimisation (SEO). It will affect how your business will appear in a search on Google or in the app store in rankings and help people to choose it. There is a cost and skill in doing this, but when using SEO you are increasing discovery without paying Google. Google would rather you pay. So, they'll try to charge you for appearing in and near key searches (paid). Apple will charge for giving you higher prominence in its app store.

Walmart makes over $3 billion annually according to Emarketer[10] (a marketing research and insights company) in 'retail media'. This is where it sells advertising and placements to products within its own online channel. They use customer and shopping behaviour data to place brand offer ads that appear more prominently as consumers shop online.

Uber now makes $1 billion in ad revenue using its data and passenger journeys to provide targeted ads and promotions. For example, 'Next time you fly from Heathrow, use Emirates.'

You can appear on social media (Facebook, TikTok, YouTube, etc.) for free by creating content for your business. Think 'How to put up shelves' for a DIY store (earned and owned) or secure a presence by paying content creators on these channels (paid and earned). Understandably, sectors like travel, fashion and beauty tend to put larger budgets into this activity, but brands across all sectors do this more and more these days. (Whether they do it well for their brand is another matter.)

LinkedIn is a significant professional network where many businesses and their employees think a presence is necessary. A B2B business may see it as a critical promotional vehicle for business audiences and target by geography, industry, job title, etc. For businesses wishing to motivate and communicate to their own staff, LinkedIn can be key for internal communications. LinkedIn and many of the channels mentioned in this chapter also allow you to pay to advertise or boost your content to increase key audience exposure.

Promotions in one area can and should be leveraged in other areas. A positive press article should be publicised in a paid social media post. A five-star review for a film must go on the poster. A discount is promoted in an ad, outbound customer emails and on the website.

Be wary of promoting the market rather than your brand. Too often, I see business promotional spend convert to sales in a competitor's favour. Häagen-Dazs had tremendous sales growth for many years and was the dominant spender on advertising in luxury ice cream. However, it was promoting the *idea* of luxury ice cream more than why Häagen-Dazs should be the luxury ice cream you choose. Both Ben & Jerry's, with its quirky flavours, and supermarket luxury own-label versions (with their lower-priced variants) benefited from the increasing demand generated by Häagen-Dazs and stole market share.

Airbnb used to spend the majority of its promotional spend on paid response advertising in digital search media. It realised it was literally paying for when people typed 'Airbnb' into Google. It now spends most of its promotion on brand advertising, PR and created content. Airbnb also uses influencers on social media. CEO Brian Chesky explained that Airbnb had woken up to the idea that marketing's role was 'to educate and not buy customers.'

How you use the 4Ps defines your brand – the Grey Goose story

If you know vodka you will know Grey Goose. Sidney Frank founded Grey Goose in the summer of 1997. At that time – and, to some extent, today – the perception was that premium vodkas had Russian origin. Some other brands with distinctive marketing had changed this. Most noticeably Absolut from Sweden had established itself around the idea of 'purity' to be seen as a premium brand worth paying more for.

Into this market came Sidney Frank. He had witnessed a boom in popularity for the premium Perrier bottled water in the USA. He decided to do the same for vodka. Grey Goose is a wholly invented brand. He made the name up first and then assembled all the marketing mix elements to redraw the vodka market in Grey Goose's favour. He invented a new category, super-premium vodka, that he then set out to own.

He sought to develop a luxury vodka and collaborated with cellar master François Thibault, who had expertise in cognac and vodka production. He wanted to create a vodka made without compromise. Grey Goose is from France and was first made in an old cognac distillery. Once created, Frank repeatedly entered it into vodka-tasting competitions. Eventually, in 1998, the Beverage Tasting Institute of Chicago conducted a blind tasting of eighty vodkas. Grey Goose came first. Frank turned this news into an ad they ran in premium lifestyle magazines. The headline was 'Rated the #1 tasting vodka in the world'. The ad then showed Grey Goose at the top of the list as number one, with the country it was made in, France, beside it. It was shown above all the other famous brands and their country of origin.

The Grey Goose brand took the idea of being a super-premium vodka into all of its 4Ps.

It was reassuringly expensive – twice the price of Absolut.

It was only available in the best bars and hotels. It took part in an event where it gave its product away for free, but this was at the *Vanity Fair* Oscars After Party. All the celebrity movie stars were seen to drink it – which, of course, Grey Goose publicised.

When it was delivered to a hotel or bar it came in wooden boxes with straw, like the best wine. It even had a cork not a screw top.

Seven years after Sidney Frank literally made up Grey Goose, he sold it to the Bacardi Group for a reported $2.2 billion.

The Grey Goose 4Ps

Product	Price
World's best-tasting vodka Super premium packaging Grain and cognac distillery Purest water Premium packaging • Cork not screw cap • Delivered in wooden boxes	Twice as expensive as its rival Never discounted
Promotion Tasting award winner PR and word-of-mouth Celebrity movie star users Exclusive and restricted ads Partnership with Vanity Fair Given away for free at Vanity Fair Oscars Party	**Place** Not readily available Best bars and hotels Best parties Originally USA and then the world

Summary

The 4Ps of marketing – product, price, place and promotion – provide a structured approach to creating the essentials of your marketing strategy. This chapter set out to open your mind to what each of the 4Ps can be in a modern world and as it continues to change.

Product. The actual goods or services being offered. A successful product fulfils an existing consumer demand or unmet need. It will stand out from competitors. It won't just be functional. It will consider design, features, branding, quality, and more.

Price. Price represents the amount charged to customers for a product or service. In a world with digital, data, and AI-connections. Price is also dynamic and behavioural. It impacts sales volume, revenue and profitability. Pricing should reflect market demand, competitor pricing, and perceived value.

Place. Where the product is sold and how it's distributed to customers. It includes distribution channels, retail locations, online platforms, and logistics. It considers customers' behaviour, their purchase journey and the best way to get products in front of the customers who are most likely to purchase them.

Promotion. A well-planned promotion strategy helps raise awareness, build brand recognition, drive engagement and persuade customers to buy. It includes advertising, social media, public relations, and sales promotions. A good way to think of promotion is paid (it costs you to get your product or service promoted), owned (you've created and own your content, like a website) and earned (doing things to appear in media, editorial or references/reviews without appearing to pay for them).

6

Making More of the Fifth P – Partnerships

You can do anything, but not everything.
DAVID ALLEN, *GETTING THINGS DONE:*
THE ART OF STRESS-FREE PRODUCTIVITY

Whether you're launching a start-up or steering an established business, partnerships can make or break your brand's reputation and growth. They have the potential to elevate your business or hinder it, depending on how they're approached.

This chapter explores how game-changing partnerships can be, offering practical guidance on creating successful ones and avoiding common pitfalls. I'll also share ten approaches to help your partnerships fly.

The power of partnerships

Partnerships are not just about shared logos or splitting profits; they can redefine how your business operates and is perceived. Done well, they become a catalyst for innovation, brand growth and market reach. Done poorly, they can harm your reputation and drain resources.

For start-ups: beyond investment

Start-ups are often consumed by the need to secure funding, but partnerships can bring so much more:

- **Industry insight:** Partners can guide start-ups through market complexities.
- **Credibility:** Aligning with an established player builds trust.
- **Market access:** Partnerships unlock new customer bases and distribution channels.
- **Technology/product integration:** Start-ups can enhance their offerings by leveraging a partner's resources.
- **Funding in kind:** Partners may provide essential services or marketing support at reduced costs.

For established brands: breaking inertia

Big brands, while secure, can become complacent. Partnerships help them inject energy and fresh thinking:

- **Reinforcing mission and values:** Partners bring complementary strengths to achieve shared goals.
- **Expanding perceptions:** Partnerships introduce brands to untapped markets or audiences.
- **Exploring new channels:** Partners open doors to new ways of reaching customers.
- **Shared interests:** Fitness, for example, links mobile, gyms, sports, insurance and more.
- **Co-creation:** Combining capabilities to develop new products or services.
- **Accelerating innovation:** Partners bring each other both a stimulus and fresh perspectives that help create new ideas.

The superpower (and kryptonite) of partnerships

When partnerships are well executed, one partner gets to borrow the other partner's marketing superpower, amplifying its reach and relevance. However, poor partnerships can have the opposite effect, damaging a brand and draining resources.

In today's world of social media and content-driven marketing, having a partnership mindset is vital. For instance, in the travel industry, social platforms and influencers play a significant role in the decision process. Not thinking about partnerships in marketing is not doing your job when:

- **77 per cent of travellers** consult at least one major platform for travel planning (Expedia).
- **75 per cent of travellers** are inspired to visit destinations they first encounter on social media (American Express Research).

Case study: Lessons from Simbiotik

Fifteen years ago, entrepreneur David Pickles founded Simbiotik, a brand partnership agency. With global agency Havas as his incubator partner, Simbiotik grew to serve major clients like PepsiCo, Levi's, Google and Sony. In 2024, Havas acquired Simbiotik, highlighting the value of strong, long-term partnerships.

Pickles identified four core benefits of partnership marketing, which he calls the 4Rs:

- **Relevance:** Borrow credibility to position your product or brand – without licensing fees.
- **Reach:** Access your partner's marketing channels – without media fees.
- **Reward:** Offer exclusive prizes or experiences to enhance campaigns – without additional costs.
- **Revenue:** Generate new income streams through licensing or joint sales – without significant overheads.

Partnerships, when approached strategically, can unlock opportunities far beyond what a business can achieve alone. They build bridges to new markets, ideas and audiences, creating value that benefits all parties involved.

In the following section, we'll dive deeper into the ten fundamentals that can help you make your partnerships soar.

10 ways to build better partnerships

1. Align your values

The cornerstone of any successful partnership is value alignment. Shared missions or philosophies resonate with audiences and ensure credibility. Misalignment, however, can lead to scepticism or reputational damage.

While many businesses have values, causes or charities they support, partnerships must transcend mere 'box-ticking'. They should reflect genuine shared goals.

CASE STUDY

Fashion brand Lacoste wanted to create a new model for sustainable fashion, minimising environmental impact. It removed its iconic crocodile logo in 2018 to spotlight ten endangered species, aligning with the International Union for Conservation of Nature (IUCN). Each limited-edition shirt was made in quantities that reflected the remaining wild population of each of the ten featured species, generating global media attention and quadrupling donations to IUCN.

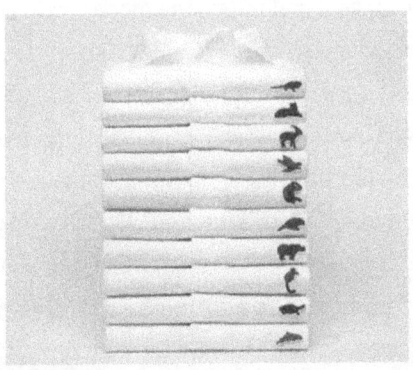

Image courtesy of IUCN

In contrast, Adidas's partnership with Kanye West for the Yeezy brand collapsed in 2022 amid controversy over West's antisemitic remarks, culminating in a high-profile fallout that tarnished both reputations.[11]

ESSENTIAL ADVICE

- Research potential partners thoroughly to ensure alignment in mission, values and audience.
- Draft a joint statement clearly outlining shared goals.
- Assess whether the partnership complements each brand's expertise, reputation and behaviour.

2. Identify overlapping audiences or interests

Successful partnerships ensure both parties' audiences align or complement each other. It makes the collaboration more natural and makes it more likely to be well received. Think beyond your own audience's journey – what other brands or experiences do they engage with?

CASE STUDY

In the 1980s, Nike pioneered a new way to do athlete partnerships by collaborating with Michael Jordan to create Air Jordan, blending brand values and audience interest. In the social media age, fans have become their own creators with huge audiences and offer a different type of engagement. The biggest golf magazine in the world is *Golf Digest*, with 1.6m subscribers and a website with 4.7m visitors. Good Good Golf is a creator fan channel on YouTube. It has over 1.75m subscribers and over 500 million views. Good Good Golf's mindset is to create partnerships with fans, players and brands. This led brands like Callaway Golf to partner with them in a seven-figure deal. Good Good Golf now sells its own products for fans via its own website. Good Good Golf uses Shopify to power their e-commerce. Shopify markets this relationship to attract other e-commerce businesses to partner with Shopify.

ESSENTIAL ADVICE
- Use tools to research audience demographics, behaviours and psychographics.
- Go where your audience is and not where it may have been.
- Design campaigns that embrace your partner's insights to better connect with your shared audience.

3. Adopt an 'explorer' mindset

To truly embrace the benefits of partnerships requires flexibility and openness. Plant seeds, water them together and let them grow a bit first to see if they are flowers or weeds. Instead of exploiting a partner's resources, adopt a collaborative, problem-solving approach. Partnerships often involve navigating challenges together, fostering innovation.

CASE STUDY

Peter Epersen was the Global Head of Crowd Sourcing and Online Innovation at LEGO. He explained to me how a partnership mindset transformed LEGO as a brand and business. Twenty years ago LEGO saw itself as 'selling bricks', with a 30 per cent year-on-year decline in sales, and was $800m in debt. LEGO transformed and became one of the world's most powerful brands. The shift was caused by a change in culture and mindset brought in by new CEO Jørgen Vig Knudstorp. He wanted people in LEGO to think like an 'explorer' rather than an 'exploiter'. 'Explorers' find new connections; 'exploiters' sell what you make. So, it inspired creativity by collaborating with fans through its LEGO Ideas platform. This crowd-sourced initiative allows fans to submit and co-create new product ideas, fostering mutual trust and changing LEGO's brand. Now we know LEGO for theme parks, movies, computer games, TV shows and much more.

ESSENTIAL ADVICE

Actively listen to your partner's perspective to find mutually beneficial solutions.

Avoid a rigid 'my way or the highway' approach; instead, co-create ideas.

Stay in the SUN: suspend (judgement), understand (your partner's perspective) and nurture (the possibilities of your partner's ideas).

4. Build an authentic story

A partnership needs a compelling narrative to create emotional resonance and avoid seeming transactional. Storytelling enhances the perceived value of the collaboration and the opportunities for media and audience engagement.

CASE STUDY

Ryan Reynolds has redefined partnership storytelling. From Aviation Gin to Wrexham AFC, his ventures incorporate humour, authenticity and community benefit. His brand collaborations have turned into cultural phenomena. He bought Wrexham AFC with Rob McElhenney and partnered with its fans and the city's wider community. This has seen Wrexham AFC rise up the league tables, become the focus of a docuseries (*Welcome to Wrexham*) and gain global media coverage. They've recently bought the brewery behind Wrexham Lager and are taking that global too. Wrexham is now bidding to become the UK City of Culture for 2029.

ESSENTIAL ADVICE

- Craft a clear, authentic narrative about the partnership.
- Develop tangible outputs – videos, articles, interviews or events – that showcase the collaboration.
- Open your mind to who might be interested in the story you have to tell – is there a trade story, an event speech, or a podcaster or opinion formers in other areas who might tell their version of your story?

5. Define and deliver mutual benefit

A partnership must provide value to all parties involved – whether through increased visibility, enhanced credibility, improved distribution or shared revenue streams. Approach partnerships with the mindset of 'what's in it for *us*?' rather than 'what's in it for me?'. A successful partnership delivers a triple win: for the brands, their audiences and other stakeholders (such as distributors and retailers).

CASE STUDY

Captain Morgan and Pepsi. This is a new co-branded product – a rum and cola drink in a can. It puts the brand names in your mind, not the generic of the mixed drink. It was perfectly timed for the Christmas 2024 season to maximise sales and delivered the mutual benefit of *new* news for both brands – whilst increasing product visibility on supermarket shelves. It increased the saliency of both brands in their audience's minds, simultaneously driving sales of the new product *and* both brands individually. The careful agreement of branding, product design and promotional campaigns underscored the partnership's success with the strapline: 'Two Greats. One Epic Taste'.

ESSENTIAL ADVICE

- Clearly outline goals and KPIs (key performance indicators) for both parties.
- Ensure fair sharing of responsibilities and resources.
- Monitor and adjust the partnership to ensure both brands enjoy sustained benefits.

6. Let loose creativity and imagination – behave like Bowie!

David Bowie's career epitomised creativity and reinvention, often through collaborations. Businesses can emulate this by treating partnerships as spaces to experiment and innovate beyond their usual boundaries. Bold, imaginative partnerships create memorable, market-defining experiences.

Case study

Red Bull and Felix Baumgartner. Few companies embrace creativity and innovation in partnerships as much as Red Bull. Its F1 team has won numerous world championships. It's created numerous original events. It supports and works with many athletes and has built one of the world's leading sports facilities in Salzburg – available to any elite athlete. One such is Felix Baumgartner, who, on 14 October 2012, ascended twenty-four miles into the stratosphere above New Mexico, suspended by a helium balloon, before taking a freefall that would test the limits of human courage and scientific understanding. The whole event – Red Bull *Stratos* – was live streamed on YouTube, capturing Baumgartner's record-breaking freefall and redefining audience engagement and brand storytelling in the process.

Essential advice

- Brainstorm unique, market-changing ideas for the partnership.
- Use innovative technologies or formats to stand out.
- Take calculated risks to surprise and delight your audience.

7. Don't ask for money – ask for advice, expertise or support

New initiatives such as launches, or scale initiatives, can be killed in businesses because they ask for money and so increase perceived risk. Partnership can enhance learning and bring in new skills and expertise that the business doesn't have to pay for. Partnerships can accelerate market entry through instant credibility, a fast track to new customer access and new innovation.

Case studies

Aldi, Channel 4 and food start-ups. Aldi is one of the biggest supermarkets but historically has been known for its value rather than its tasty food. Through *The Next Big Thing* TV series, Aldi gave small food and drinks start-ups exposure and coaching. In return, Aldi gained publicity and exclusive, innovative products for its shelves. Each show saw companies pitch their new product ideas, with only one winner making it onto the shelves.

Uber and Toyota. When Uber was growing as a business, it needed to expand its fleet. It partnered with Toyota to offer a leasing programme for Uber drivers, reducing up-front costs for Uber and introducing Toyota to a new customer base.

ESSENTIAL ADVICE

- Don't just look for money. Seek partners with complementary skills or resources that fill your gaps.
- Look to create partnerships where both parties bring unique strengths, thus reducing costs.

8. Accelerate innovation

Partnership can spark innovation by combining the creative capabilities, expertise and technologies of both parties. This allows businesses to solve problems or explore opportunities faster than they could do on their own.

CASE STUDY

NASA and Black & Decker. To get to the moon NASA had to solve a lot of problems. You'd naturally associate NASA with science genius and innovation. Yet, it sought expertise and innovation from brands including IBM, Goodyear, Whirlpool, Dupont and Black & Decker. NASA's partnership with Black & Decker arose from trying to resolve how to drill or collect rocks without a cable. So, NASA briefed Black & Decker on its problem. It got a solution it took to the moon. Black & Decker got the innovation that led to the first handheld vacuum cleaner, the Dustbuster. NASA took the Black & Decker brand beyond the market for tools and to a new audience.

ESSENTIAL ADVICE

- Identify the partner companies that can enhance your product or service through technology or the expertise you need.
- Work out what are the best joint-innovation areas to solve shared problems or create new opportunities, such as creating a new feature or entering a niche market.
- Work out and plan for the long term who gets what and what are the terms of the venture.

9. Seek competitive advantage

Because partnerships can create unique value propositions, they differentiate a start-up from its competitors or give a major brand an edge in a noisy or crowded market. Your initiative should not be something that can be hijacked or leveraged by your competition.

CASE STUDY

Hotel and influencer partnerships: Mandarin Oriental Hotels defines itself as the ultimate in luxury. Its long-running 'I'm a Fan' campaign features celebrities like Morgan Freeman and Dame Helen Mirren. The partnership was not just an exchange of money for celebrity endorsement. Only a limited number of 'true fans' of Mandarin Oriental were asked to participate. They aren't paid. Instead, they were contracted to be able to stay at Mandarin hotels and given support by Mandarin for their charity activities. The large number of A-list celebrities who were genuine fans ensured no other hotel brand could compete in this way. Mandarin Oriental achieved the highest brand awareness in its sector and revenue grew 800 per cent.

ESSENTIAL ADVICE

- Look for partnerships that offer something unique or exclusive.
- Contractually safeguard the partnership to prevent competitors from leveraging your efforts or stealing your idea.

- If you can create clear space against the competition by being first or having unique access, make sure you own it and use it to your advantage.

10. Establish transparent success metrics

Your version of what success looks like is unlikely to be the same as your partner. You don't want to be a year into a relationship to discover you are on a different page. You are better off finding out early where there are any gaps in aspirations or expectations. Then you can deal with them when they first appear. You can look for ways around them. If what is expected from either party is seen as unachievable, walk away before time, energy and money have been invested. Trust is the foundation of any partnership. Both partners must establish shared goals, open communication and transparency to ensure smooth collaboration.

ESSENTIAL ADVICE

- Define shared goals and performance indicators early.
- Establish clear communication channels for collaboration.
- Regularly review and adjust the partnership's direction.

Summary

Partnerships have been fundamental to big names like NASA, Red Bull, LEGO, Pepsi and Ryan Reynolds. They've all benefited from the 4Rs: relevance, reach, reward, revenue.

Done well, partnerships can bring industry insight, credibility, market access, technology/product integration, funding in kind, expanding perceptions, exploring new channels, co-creation and accelerating innovation. Consider partnership the fifth P. Whether you are a start-up or an established business, don't ignore how partnerships could redefine how your business operates and is perceived.

7

Removing the Confusion Between
Purpose, Mission and Vision

*When you are a Bear of Very Little Brain, and you Think of Things,
you find sometimes that a Thing which seemed very Thingish inside
you is quite different when it gets out into the open and has other
people looking at it.*

A.A. MILNE, *THE HOUSE AT POOH CORNER*, 1928

So, what does a brand's purpose, mission and vision actually mean, and
how should you develop them?

Marketing would probably be better understood if the word
'purpose' was banned. People often say purpose when they actually
mean mission, vision or values. Mission, vision and values all have
specific meanings for a reason. When communication and
understanding are confused, the chances of building a coherent brand
go with them.

It Began with *Start with Why*

Simon Sinek, with his hugely popular book, *Start with Why*, was a
catalyst for the obsession with purpose in business.

The thing is that when Simon Sinek explains his 'Start with Why'
concept, he uses Apple as an example. Apple is a very different business
in how it thinks and runs compared to most others. In *Start with Why*,
Sinek codifies what he calls the Golden Circle. He explains that many
organisations go about what they do the wrong way round.

1.   WHAT? (What the business does)
2.   HOW? (How the business does it)
3.   WHY? (What is your purpose, cause or belief)

He's right: WHAT and HOW are more common in business, while WHY is rarer in business.

Sinek is clear: WHY is not to make a profit. For a small number of businesses, like Patagonia and indeed Movember, the concept of 'Start with Why' and having a 'purpose' can be a compelling idea. However, these are exceptional brands.

Many brands are confused about how their purpose is not to just make a profit. Yet, the trend towards WHY resulted in what became a populist business bandwagon for the desire for 'purpose' whilst also not really being sure what it meant. What many thought purpose meant was shifting their business to a public focus to be seen to be *doing public good* as their reason for being – whether it was insurance, technology, air travel or making cakes. In the process, marketing and what business is about got very confused. Businesses also started to pretend and game what good they were doing. For example, companies would cherry-pick information and pretend to be more environmentally friendly than they really were. In many instances, rather than it being genuine they got trapped in box-ticking brand behaviour.

If you want to do good, put it in your mission, values and your corporate governance

There is nothing wrong with a company wanting to do good. That's what Patagonia clothing does. But they say in their mission statement, 'We are in the business to save the planet'. But then 'purpose' became a bandwagon and mutated into corporate hypocrisy. Business and marketing suffered from 'purpose FOMO' (fear of missing out). Lots of organisations and marketers wanted to show they had a purpose. If it made working in business and the world better, I could live with the confusion. But as I look at current world events, it doesn't seem to have made things better.

Following the death of George Floyd and the rise of the Black Lives Matter movement, a number of companies championed that they would have a 'purpose' to actively promote DEI (diversity, equity and inclusion). In 2022, McKinsey & Company reported that companies with robust DEI programmes were benefiting as businesses. They were better able to respond to challenges, win in demand talent and meet the needs of different customer bases.[12]

I'm a great believer in the business benefits of DEI. There is a lot of evidence to prove it. A number of companies seemed to agree in 2019 and publicise this as their 'purpose' or in their 'values'. Only five years later, many of those same companies now appear to be going in the opposite direction. Ford, Harley-Davidson, Molson Coors, Jack Daniels, Amazon, Google and Meta have all recently said they are abandoning or rolling back DEI initiatives.[13] It's probably not a coincidence that this coincided with Donald Trump being re-elected. Possibly they are pragmatically bowing to pressure to conceal those beliefs for now? That still raises the question of how genuine that claimed purpose or those values were in the first place.

Consumers are cynical about company purpose

In 2021, I ran a quantified survey in the UK. It revealed that in that year, 58 per cent of people believed most businesses making claims they are spending more time and money marketing their environmental and societal intentions were greenwashing.

So, what should marketing do now that it's:

- Got itself confused about what purpose means,
- Taking contradictory actions,
- Disbelieved by consumers?

In my view: carry on with the desire to do good. Do even more that's good for the planet and embrace diversity, equity and inclusion. Make consumers aware of it, but to avoid any confusion and increased cynicism, publish it as an open 'commitment' and be transparent about how you'll measure achieving it. If you are a company that is about having a 'purpose' and doing good at your core, I salute you. The smart thing to do for most other businesses is to go back to your knitting – your marketing. Understand, define and then live your real mission, vision and values.

Mission

I advise any founders I work with to start by defining their business's mission. I typically do this by asking them questions, challenging their answers and extracting from these exchanges what really matters.

I'll often start by asking each leadership team member some questions individually. The moment they all see where they agree, disagree or have different views is frequently eye-opening – if the leadership team disagrees, it should ring alarm bells.

What is a mission?

A mission is the grit in the oyster when the business started. It's the thing they reacted to that annoys them and motivates them to produce its pearl.

Your mission statement answers the question: Why does my business exist?

The mission declares what your company sets out to do. It's the standard against which you weigh your actions and your decisions. Mission relates to what you promise to accomplish for your clients. It is beyond the making of money or gaining market share.

YOUR MISSION IS YOUR 'WHY?' AND YOUR 'WHAT?'

Ideally, a mission captures what inspires your plans and drives your actions and those of the people working in your business. Technically, your mission statement should include a definition of your primary customers, identify the products and services you produce and describe the geographical location where you operate.

YOUR MISSION IS YOUR NORTH STAR

The mission statement should be very clear. It provides the company with direction and focus. It helps you find the right customers ... typically also your most profitable customers. It should remind any company member what everyone is trying to achieve, and they should all be able to recall it. It is something they live and breathe – the internal and external driver in how the business interacts with prospects, customers, media, partners and associates.

Mission statements go beyond the 'to-do' list

They are what keep people and the company on track. To get to a mission statement, ask and answer basic questions like:

- For whom do we do what we do?
- Why do we serve our clients in the way that we do?
- How do we serve our clients in the way that we do?
- Why are we in this industry?
- Why did we start this business?
- What image of our business do we want to convey?

When writing a mission statement, create dynamic, visual images that inspire action. Describe the mission using unusual, colourful verbs and language. A great mission statement will draw your dream clients towards you. People, internally and externally, should get excited about what they and you are doing.

Here are some examples:

Amazon: To be Earth's most customer-centric company.

eBay: To provide a global trading platform where practically anyone can trade practically anything.

Google: To organise the world's information and make it universally accessible and useful.

Instagram: To capture and share the world's moments.

Kickstarter: To bring creative projects to life.

LinkedIn: To connect the world's professionals to make them more productive and successful.

Nike: To bring inspiration and innovation to every athlete in the world.

Patagonia: To be in business to save our home planet.

Shopify: To make commerce better for everyone.

TED: To spread ideas.

Tesla: To accelerate the world's transition to sustainable energy.

Uber: To reimagine the way the world moves for the better.

An example of creating a mission: Dollar Shave Club

Michael Dubin was working dead-end jobs. He met Mark Levine at a party. They bonded over their shared hatred of razor prices. There must be a better way. So, with just $35,000, they decided to take on Gillette. Gillette makes razors expensive and hard to buy. People dreaded going in-store to buy razors and pay a fortune for something that should be simple. So Dubin and Levine wrote a comedy script and called some improv friends. They shot the now-famous video (look it up – if you haven't seen it) called 'Our Blades are F***ing Great'. Twelve thousand orders flooded in. They had also entirely rethought how razors are sold. Not in shops, but online and delivered to your home. There was more than enough margin between what Gillette charged and what they could produce great razors for. It was hard for Gillette to fight back – without disrupting its brand and model.

It's unlikely Dollar Shave Club wrote down their mission at the time. However, they had one that motivated them – the grit in their oyster. Dollar Shave Club was sold to Unilever in 2016 for $1 billion. Unilever now describes Dollar Shave Club's mission as follows: 'Our mission is to provide high-quality razors and grooming products at an affordable price, delivered conveniently to our customers' doorsteps.'

Remember, this is after Unilever. It's technically correct but a bit corporate and not vibrant or exciting. You can't help but think that, had Dubin and Levine written one at the time, it would have a bit more edge and possibly more swearing. Something more like: 'Our mission is to cut the crap and add some fun to getting loads more people great razors at great value.'

Vision

What's your future? Having identified your mission, you can then stretch it forward. If you are successful in your mission, imagine what you could achieve. A vision looks ten years out. Unleash your big, audacious imagination. A vision statement answers the question, 'Where do I see my business going?'

What is a vision?

- Vision is the difference your business will make in your customers' lives or the wider world if you ultimately realise your mission.

- Vision statements are future-based and are meant to inspire and give direction to the company's employees, not necessarily anyone outside the company.
- A vision is usually qualitative but still grounded in reality rather than a complete dream. If it can be quantified – especially into something tangible – all the better.

When planning the space programme in the 1960s, NASA defined its vision: 'To boldly expand frontiers in air and space for the benefit of the USA and to inspire and improve the quality of life on earth.' This was quantified in a President Kennedy speech 'that the US should commit itself to achieving the goal, before this decade is out, of landing a man on the Moon and returning him safely to the Earth'.

A good vision statement usually . . .

- Is easy for employees to understand and rally around.
- Is something that can last five to ten years or more.
- Will have a nice tension between aspiration (stretch) and reality (achievement).
- Dreams big and paints a picture.
- Focuses on success.
- Uses the present tense.
- Has passion and emotion.

You can also add to this list 'Has a financial positioning element' – but I prefer not to. It could aim to be number one in your area, but I encourage people to think beyond this.

A vision statement isn't . . .

- A positioning statement.
- Something we've already achieved.
- *How* we get there. (It is ... 'Where could we be?')

- Long-winded and unmemorable. (People should be able to remember it and describe it in an elevator.)

Visions are long-term but can change over time

Companies grow, objectives and goals may change. Microsoft's vision used to be: 'A personal computer in every home running Microsoft software.' It was relevant and inspiring a while back but isn't anymore. Visions should be written in a way that lasts years rather than months.

Vision examples:

IKEA: To create a better everyday life for the many people.

Oxfam: A just world without poverty.

San Diego Zoo: To become a world leader in connecting people to wildlife and conservation.

WWF: We seek to save a planet, a world of life. Reconciling the needs of human beings and the needs of others that share the Earth.

Tesla: To create the most compelling car company of the twenty-first century by driving the world's transition to electric vehicles.

Here are two simple things you can do to help craft a vision statement:

1. Finish a sentence that begins: 'We will ...'

2. When you have some draft vision statements, torture-test them to improve them. You do this by looking at the statement and asking the question, 'Will it inspire people?'

I suggest you start with your mission and then work out your vision. Once you've done both, you should check back.

Your mission statement should clarify what you want to achieve, who for and why you'll do it.

A vision statement describes where you want to take these people, or the world, as a result of delivering what you do.

The vision is an ultimate imagined possible destination. The mission is the road map you can use today to get there.

8

Values Matter, but Mind the Gap

A principle is not a principle until it costs you money.
BILL BERNBACH, FOUNDER OF ADVERTISING AGENCY DDB
(DOYLE DANE BERNBACH)

Brand values are the central beliefs that guide a company's actions, decisions and interactions with customers, employees and the community. They are a fundamental part of a company's identity. They should be reflected in the company's strategy, behaviour, culture and messaging. When using words as values, they are things like precision, innovation, open-mindedness, curiosity, bravery, plain speaking, etc.

What are values?
- Your values are your belief system or your principles for your brand and business.
- Whether you work for a start-up or an established business, imagine defining the five to seven principles your company and its people adhere to, which also matter.
- Values guide a company and its staff's approach to how it goes about acting and communicating. They point out how to deal with things when good or bad happens.

Why values matter
- Values create a sense of cohesion and direction for a company and a brand.

- They help attract the best talent.
- They provide compelling glue and grip for how people in a business work.

What do values do?

- They define a company's identity. They shape how it is perceived and what it stands for.
- They show what's important to the company. Values represent what the company embodies, beyond what its products or services do.
- They guide decision-making. Values help leaders make strategic decisions referring back to core principles.
- They create a lasting impression. Values that are true and followed through in actions and behaviours differentiate a company from its competitors.

Full statements for values are preferable to just using individual words. Values can be defined as individual words, but turning them into sentences or mantras by which a company lives is more meaningful. For example, 'integrity' is a value – but what does that mean? It's better to say: 'We keep our promises. We do the right thing by our clients and each other.'

CASE STUDY

Patagonia has the best business reputation in America and has the top market share in the outdoor apparel market. Living up to its commitment to sustainability can be challenging. It has involved decades of admitting flaws, solving problems and finding ways of bringing along suppliers, employees and customers. Now, 100 per cent of the electricity in its US facilities is from renewable sources and 98 per cent of Patagonia's product lines use recycled materials.

Patagonia only has five defined values. Are the values retrofitted to its performance? No! Living those values drives their achievements and makes them different from other businesses.

- **Quality:** Build the best product, provide the best service and constantly improve everything we do.
- **Integrity:** Examine our practices openly and honestly, learn from our mistakes and meet our commitments.
- **Environmentalism:** Protect our home planet.
- **Justice:** Be just, equitable and antiracist as a company and in our community.
- **Not bound by convention:** Do it our way. Our success – and much of the fun – lies in developing new ways to do things.

On the Patagonia website, after each value there is additional copy. After the 'quality' value it reads: 'The best product is useful, versatile, long-lasting, repairable and recyclable. Our ideal is regenerative products that give back to the earth as much as they take.' Feels like there's substance behind it.

Case study: When values are lived and when they are a lie – SSE vs Boeing

SSE (Scottish & Southern Energy) is a major energy company in the UK. It distributes energy to homes and businesses and is responsible for maintaining energy infrastructure in key regions. Boeing is one of the world's major aerospace companies that develops, manufactures and services commercial aeroplanes, defence products and space systems.

Both SSE and Boeing share the brand value 'safety'. You can understand, given what they do, why this value matters. But it's hard to find a more extreme example of when a value is lived and when it is allowed to become a lie. Let's start with Boeing.

SAFETY AS A VALUE AT BOEING

Boeing used to be synonymous with innovation and safety in aviation. It produced planes like the 747 Jumbo Jet. However, Boeing's brand reputation has been compromised by a string of high-profile mechanical failures, management errors and safety concerns.

Boeing's Starliner spacecraft was involved in an incident that left NASA astronauts Suni Williams and Butch Wilmore stranded in space. There were two fatal crashes of Boeing's 737 MAX aircraft in 2018 and 2019. This led to 346 people being killed and the plane being grounded for nearly two years. Boeing's corporate culture and decision-making processes chased profits over being true to its values.[14]

A key business decision failure was outsourcing 70 per cent of their design and manufacturing to over fifty suppliers worldwide, where it was poorly supervised. It pursued a profit mindset and took engineering values out of the heart of the brand.

Boeing agreed to plead guilty in US courts to fraud in the 737 incidents. Victims' relatives called for Boeing's executives to be charged with negligence. According to Morning Consult Brand Intelligence, there has been a massive decline in trust in Boeing. In February 2024, it was only 14 per cent for frequent flyers. Passengers are now checking what make of plane they are on rather than just the airline. Boeing's share price has crashed, with the *Financial Times* describing it as 'among the US's foremost corporate dumpster fires'.[15]

SAFETY AS A VALUE AT SSE

I remember going to my first meeting in Perth, Scotland, when I was working with SSE. They explained that safety wasn't just a value for an SSE engineer. It was a company-wide value. They told me:

- Never to run.
- Always to hold handrails when walking down stairs.

- If you parked a car, reverse in as it minimises accidents compared to reversing out.
- Don't speed when driving.
- If anybody in the company saw someone breaking these behaviours, regardless of their position, they were expected to call them out.

I freely admit that when I was inducted, my reaction was that this was over the top as I wouldn't be working outside. I'd walk down stairs and forget to hold a handrail. People would politely call me out. After a while you got used to it. They made me aware and made me think about how I behaved safely. Safety was not just a written value; it was embedded in the culture at SSE. They held safety conferences and visited schools. Whether you drove a van, worked in an office or were a linesman climbing an electricity pole, they challenged and evaluated themselves on safety from the Chief Executive down.

If you were working on an electricity pole when the pressure might be on to get the job done, they were clear your priority was to behave safely:

- If in doubt, stop the job.
- Look out for everyone.
- Do walk, don't run.
- Danger? Speak up!
- Reverse park your car.

Safety at SSE was a company-wide in-built attitude of mind and behaviour. It makes commitments like spending £2.5m alone on its Perth Safety Training Centre. That's why SSE was the UK's safest power company. It's difficult to understand how my holding a handrail meant fewer people getting injured and dying across the business. Yet, somehow, it did.

The failures at Boeing show the dangers of a gap between 'claimed' and 'actual' in a company's values. Yet, for many businesses, values are something the board says matter. They wordsmith values but don't follow through to make them real.

Untrue values are often an early warning sign for a company failure

I've witnessed companies claim a value of 'innovation' where nobody is willing to share an idea for fear of being told that it is wrong. I've seen companies with 'collaboration' as a value where the business is run in siloed departments all targeted by management to deliver different KPIs.

Research indicates many companies have stated values they don't live. MIT Sloan released a study in 2019[16] where they reviewed the websites and annual reports of 689 large, mainly US organisations.

- 80 per cent of major US companies have published values.
- Integrity was the most common value, listed by 65 per cent of all companies, followed by collaboration (53 per cent), customer focus (48 per cent), and respect (35 per cent).
- However, when data from the 2019 Culture 500 via Glass Door employee ratings[17] is compared with company-claimed values, it shows no correlation between the values a company espouses in its official corporate culture and how well it lives up to those values in employees' eyes.

A large number of company values have corporate vanity not brand truth. This is because values are too often seen as something to get done and dusted. They are written to allow organisations to have a corporate veneer – the values exist only to convey a sense of credibility. Too many companies sign off values which the leadership and the people in the business don't live by.

How to spot value gaps

If a new CEO (Chief Executive Officer) or CMO (Chief Marketing Officer) arrives at a company, they should check the claimed values. Then do independent (anonymised) research with their staff, customers and retailers.

You should ask them to spontaneously suggest words, phrases and statements about the business and what values they think guide its behaviour.

Additionally, you should create a series of statements or words (including the existing values) and ask respondents to score them from 1–10 (where 10 is excellent).

Now you have a quick snapshot of the perceived scores for your values (as well as other potential values). You can see the strengths, weaknesses and gaps. You can see how customer or retailer perceptions differ from those inside the business.

An interesting exercise is to see how perceptions of values differ around the business; for example, the board vs all staff or those in the company for five plus years vs recent joiners.

Taking action from a value gap analysis

If you find a gap between claimed values and actual behaviour, alarm bells should ring. Your job should then be to fix those gaps. Ask yourself if the area where the gap exists matters. Few businesses are great in all the places they'd like to be. You can't fix everything at once. Park it for later if it's not a priority area. If the value does matter and you have a gap, the one thing you can't do is ignore it. You must dig deeper into the root cause of the gap. Sometimes, people don't know what the company is doing. You are doing innovative things, but you've never told them. Sometimes, it's due to historical processes and behaviours that could be refined or changed. If so, change them.

If there is a significant gap in important values, you must take action to fix it. To do that, you must do three things:

1. Be open about the issue. Explain the gap in values and why you think it exists.
2. Be clear about why you think these values matter.
3. Explain what you are planning to do to fix it and by when. Not just in words but in actions.

When you are developing company brand values, avoid these five common mistakes.

1. **Lack of independent open evaluation:** The environment for evaluating current values or developing new ones must avoid corporate pressure and group thinking.
2. **Wordsmithing and spin:** People often get obsessed with language rather than meaning. The value of 'authentic' is a popular one. In my experience, few can define what they mean by it.
3. **Values that are generic and category hygiene factors**: You want values that are true to your business but also make you different from your competition. I did a workshop with the board of a global insurance company reviewing their current values. We also reviewed competitors' claimed values and watched endless repeats of 'integrity', 'customer first', 'honest', 'excellence' and 'innovation'. You'd expect an insurance company to be 'honest'. You'd hope they have 'integrity', and if you thought they didn't put the 'customer first' you might not choose them. As words they conjure up a generic response for the market of 'Well, you would say that, wouldn't you?' Companies need to ask themselves harder questions to determine what matters more to them and makes them distinctive rather than part of a herd.
4. **Values claimed are not credible.** Companies pick values they want to have but which are not true (e.g., collaborative, innovative). If the values are things the company wants to work

with in the future, explain internally why this value needs to be introduced and have a plan for change. If not, credibility in the value is lost.

5. **Leadership out of touch with staff and customers.** Too many in leadership don't see how the business works from the perspective of their customers or those who work inside the business.

Summary

Brand values are the central beliefs that guide a company's actions, decisions and interactions with customers, employees and the community. Patagonia shows how powerful strong and consistent values can be for:

- Building trust and loyalty.
- Differentiating a business from its competitors.
- Creating emotional bonds with consumers.
- Attracting the best customers and employees.
- Providing a focus for consistency in messaging and actions and better ways to navigate crises and challenges when they arise.

Untrue values are often an early warning sign for a company's future failure. Boeing's casual attitude to the value of safety saw planes fall from the sky and its market value crash as well. Yet research shows that, for many companies, there is no correlation between what they claim their values are and what their staff believe. More marketers and boards urgently need to learn how to assess and develop values properly. More importantly, the growing trend to values as something to tickbox, manipulate or use as flags of convenience a company hides behind to mitigate its actual behaviours, must stop.

When Brands Go Wrong

If you can't say it to someone's face without
feeling embarrassed, don't say it.
DAVE DYE, AWARD-WINNING ADVERTISING CREATIVE DIRECTOR[18]

Remember: 'A brand is what it does', and 'A brand is what people say when you are not in the room'. The history of marketing is littered with brands that never got that memo. Not paying attention to these fundamental truths creates confusion, reputational damage and business failure.

There are some common brand mistakes in this chapter. I've listed the failures to watch out for, with examples from the past and present. These mistakes will continue in the future – as we are in a digital, data and AI world, we will find new ways to make them. Just try to make sure it isn't you who does.

Live in the real world, not 'marketing la-la land'

Every marketer would benefit from a Post-it note stuck on their laptop that reads, 'Remember – you are not the target audience!' Here are some examples of marketing fails.

CASE STUDY: H&M: 'COOLEST MONKEY IN THE JUNGLE' HOODIE

In 2018, Swedish company H&M designed and produced a children's hoodie. They advertised it featuring a black child with the slogan 'Coolest monkey in the jungle' on its website. Critics labelled the campaign as racially insensitive. This led to calls for boycotts.[19] This was not the first time H&M had done racially offensive marketing.[20] To protect the brand from further damage, it hired a diversity leader. It issued a public apology on its website. It would be better to have a culture that spotted this in the first place.

CASE STUDY: BRITISH AIRWAYS TAILFIN FIASCO

In the late 1990s, British Airways wanted to be seen to be more international and broaden its appeal. The marketing idea was to replace all the BA Union Jack tail designs with a variety of abstract global art. This ploy succeeded in generating global PR. But out in the real world, there was no brand consistency in what a BA plane looked like. The change alienated their loyal customers and did little to attract international customers. Politicians and passengers criticised it. BA threw away years of building recognisable brand iconography because nobody considered the emotional connection that existed with national or cultural symbols.

Failure to understand your audience's needs, preferences or challenges

This is the fast track to brand irrelevance. Identifying a gap in the market doesn't mean there is a market in the gap. Brands get too excited about their new idea or too close to what they already do. They fail to stand back and ask themselves if what they are doing is meeting an unmet need or offering distinct benefits that solve people's problems.

CASE STUDY: BLACKBERRY'S FAILURE TO ADAPT TO CHANGING AUDIENCE NEEDS

Blackberry was once the dominant mobile device in business. However, its brand developed around a rigid set of selling points about the security of its closed platform. It saw itself as the mobile business machine that typed emails and messages on the move. It didn't look to innovate outside of its existing bubble of thought for what the market wanted. It dismissed the threat of the iPhone. It saw the price Apple wanted to charge as too high for a consumer device. It saw business use as the premium market. Rather than seeing a touchscreen from the audience's perspective, it saw it as *not* offering a keyboard. When businesses and consumers actively embraced cloud-based and collaborative mobiles, Blackberry became irrelevant. According to Statista, in the UK in December 2011 Blackberry had a 33.2 per cent share of smartphone sales. Two years later in 2013 it had almost halved to 17.44 per cent. By 2021 it was effectively 0 per cent.

CASE STUDY: WHAT GOOGLE GLASS DIDN'T SEE COMING

Google's futuristic eyewear Google Glass was launched to massive publicity in 2013. Google got sucked into the wonders of the possibilities of wearing glasses that could film people, go on the internet and more. Few people inside Google or its marketing team thought from the general audience's perspective, i.e., 'people are filming me without my permission'. Privacy concerns arose, along with a belief that this was all a little bit creepy. People started to think differently about what Google was doing. Google learned from the technology, but Google Glass was discontinued in 2023.

Becoming the category generic rather than a distinctive brand

Being first to market in a product area should be an advantage, yet brand history is littered with firsts to market that failed. MySpace came before Facebook, Napster before Spotify, AltaVista before Google and Nokia before Apple. Being first means little if you don't build a compelling value proposition and join up your 4Ps. Brands can create or make a market but then become redundant when their competitors develop more distinctive offerings.

CASE STUDY: TIVO – WHEN AWARENESS DOESN'T HAVE A VALUE PROPOSITION

TiVo was the first digital video recorder (DVR) in 1999. It allowed you to pause live TV, skip commercials and record shows. TiVo became a phenomenon. TiVo even became a verb synonymous with recording TV. TiVo sold its innovation in boxes with a subscription. It had millions of subscribers and was seen as a game changer. However, TiVo got its brand positioning wrong. It sold as a premium standalone product with high up-front costs and monthly fees. This limited its market. It pivoted too late to build a tech brand and license its tech to the market. A tech brand or what is known as an 'ingredient' brand strategy is used by the likes of Gore-Tex in clothing or Intel in computers. The 'Intel inside' campaign for years positioned it as the premium computer chip that a variety of hardware manufacturers were happy to buy and promote. In the case of TiVo, competitors quickly bundled DVRs with affordable cable and satellite TV packages. TiVo became a cautionary marketing tale.

Over-promising and under-delivering

As a rule, it is better in marketing to under-promise and overdeliver. A pleasant surprise is better than being let down or disappointed. These days, with sophisticated logistics, data and algorithms, businesses are trying to maximise the delivery of what they promise in all sorts of ways. Transparency in access to information and openly managing and dealing with expectations is vital. If you have some control of a market, like seats on a plane, you can abuse that power for profit. But the morals and ethics of doing this are debatable. Having a customer buy from you despite hating you is not a good place to be. When a customer can eventually buy elsewhere, they probably will.

CASE STUDY: HERMES – A BRAND WITH SUCH A BAD REPUTATION THAT IT HAD TO CHANGE ITS NAME

Hermes was one of the most successful delivery companies in the UK, taking on established players. It had significant growth. It was among the earliest businesses to deploy the 'gig economy' idea – outsourcing delivery to an army of self-employed agents incentivised to hit delivery numbers. However, these targets combined with poor logistics and awful customer service. Hermes was plagued with failures and complaints. Even though the business was looking to drastically overhaul how it operated, its brand reputation was so bad that people didn't believe it would change.[21] It decided it had no choice but to change its name to Evri as a signal of transformation. However, the depth of the poor reputation meant this change was treated with cynicism. It continued to face complaints and ridicule with tweets like 'Now we can say my parcel is missing evri tim'.[22]

CASE STUDY: HOOVER FLIGHTS TO DISASTER

In the 1990s, Hoover ran a promotional device to boost flagging sales. The offer mechanic was that customers buying a minimum of £100 of Hoover products would qualify for two return flights to the USA. Hoover got the mathematics of the level of consumer response wrong. Rather than persuading just some consumers to spend more with Hoover, it was perceived as a great-value way for anyone to get two US flights for just £100 with a free vacuum cleaner. Hoover cancelled the promotion after consumers had already bought the products. Reneging on the offer resulted in protests and legal action. It was disastrous for the eighty-four-year-old company. It led to the loss of Hoover's Royal Warrant after a 2004 BBC documentary was screened. The European branch of the company was sold to one of its competitors.[23]

Forgetting that consistency is the essence of great brands

You are building a brand because it builds trust, reinforces recognition and increases loyalty. Think of the personal or business relations you have. If people are inconsistent or unpredictable, you become uncertain about how to deal with them or what to expect. The same is true for brands. Consistency in identity, message and experience across all touchpoints makes a brand more memorable and dependable to its audience. If you've established brand trust and your audience has positive associations inside their head, only disrupt them if you have an excellent reason.

CASE STUDY: WAS UBER PREMIUM, AFFORDABLE OR TO BE TRUSTED?

Uber's initial identity was as a luxury ride service. However, in 2012 it introduced UberX as a more affordable option. Uber was chasing aggressive expansion in every direction. In 2014 it added Uber for Business aimed at also capturing the corporate travel market. It's possible for a brand to crack democratising quality with value – like an Ikea. However, at the time, Uber was being led by its gung-ho co-founder Travis Kalanick. Uber didn't have a Chief Marketing Officer, and it showed. Uber was simultaneously introducing both brand dilution and confusion. Was it offering luxury, affordability or a corporate service? In reality, there was no difference in the type of driver or car you would get with UberX or Uber for Business. They came from the same driver pool. Imagine if an airline offered business and economy and there was no difference to the seat or experience. If Uber was attempting to be perceived as premium for corporate customers, it wasn't sending out those signals. NBC News described in an article 'Ubers Wild 2014' a service that included strikes, protests, lawsuits, accusations of poor driver checks, allegations of drivers kidnapping and rapes. Whilst Uber continued to expand, it did so against a rising tide of negative publicity. There was mounting criticism of its confusing brand associations and negative corporate culture by experts and shareholders. In 2017, pressure from five of Uber's investors forced Kalanick to step down as CEO.

CASE STUDY: THE UNREAL THING – 'NEW COKE'

It's unbelievable that someone in marketing ever did this. Still, in the early 1980s, Coca-Cola faced growing competition from Pepsi, which was running a campaign with a 'Pepsi taste challenge'. Coca-Cola clearly didn't understand the sentiment and loyalty towards its own brand. So, in 1985, they reformulated the ninety-nine-year-old recipe to create a sweeter version of Coca-Cola. It launched New Coke. New Coke was designed to taste better when tasted next to Pepsi. However, loyal Coke drinkers felt betrayed by the change from their beloved original formula. A cultural icon was being tampered with and destroying its identity. Coca-Cola received thousands of calls and was mocked in the media. Some consumers began hoarding old Coke. Just seventy-nine days later the Coca-Cola original was brought back with the marketing 'save' of calling it 'Coca-Cola Classic'. Coke restored some of its brand credibility.

Losing control of brand delivery

In chasing growth and revenue, brands can look for commercial efficiencies. It begins by outsourcing to third parties, or by franchising the brand and letting other organisations trade on the name. The danger is that these 'others' aren't vested in and trained on the brand. The pursuit of cost efficiency can hollow out a brand.

CASE STUDY: JAMIE'S ITALIAN – A PERSONAL BRAND STRETCHED TOO FAR

Jamie Oliver is a famous chef who became a food and restaurant brand. Oliver and his food associations were things like friendly, accessible, good, straightforward, fresh and cooked with care and passion. Oliver extended his brand into a chain of Jamie's Italian restaurants. He said his brand mission was 'to positively disrupt mid-market dining in the high street in the UK with great value and much higher-quality ingredients, best-in-class animal welfare standards and an amazing team'.

As it expanded, those running the restaurants didn't have the same standards as Oliver. Ten years after opening, writing in *The Sunday Times*, Marina O'Loughlin's verdict on the tagliatelle with truffles at

Jamie's in Westfield Stratford was: 'Appalling, a honking, salty swamp of a sauce, brown and dusty with nutmeg. Tiny chunks, not shavings, of tasteless black truffle lurk around, like mouse poop in soup.'[24] Eight months after this review, Jamie's restaurant chain was in administration.

Lack of crisis planning and management

Shit happens. You can't always predict it. However, if you plan ahead you can work out what you might do. You are also less likely to have a problem in the first place. When a crisis does happen, you'll know how to manage it to minimise brand-reputation damage. Slow and opaque brand management in a crisis can be catastrophic.

CASE STUDY: UNITED AIRLINES PASSENGER REMOVAL

In 2017, United Airlines overbooked a flight. A passenger on board the plane didn't want to leave. So, the staff got security to forcibly remove him. The incident was videoed and then shared online. United faced a significant social and media backlash. They made the issue worse. CEO Oscar Munoz described the passenger as 'disruptive and belligerent',[25] passing the blame onto him rather than addressing United's role in causing the situation. The video triggered widespread outrage. Shortly after, the value of United's holding company fell by $1 billion.[26]

Relying solely on data as the answer and losing the emotional connection

Insights from data and machine-learning algorithms can be invaluable. But mistakes can be hard to reverse when they damage trust in your brand, so get a human to oversee the insights and apply critical thinking to what is being done. This is more important than ever for brands.

CASE STUDY: EQUIFAX ISN'T EQUITABLE

Between 17 March and 6 April 2022, Equifax issued inaccurate credit scores to major lenders for millions of consumers applying for loans, mortgages and credit cards. Credit scores were significantly wrong for over 300,000 people. This affected interest rates charged and led to rejected loans. Equifax dismissively blamed it on a 'coding issue'. An exposé broke in the *Wall Street Journal*. Equifax stock fell by 5 per cent. It was also hit with a class action lawsuit led by a Florida resident denied an auto loan after Equifax told the lender her credit score was 130 points lower than it should have been.[27]

CASE STUDY: McDONALD'S AI DRIVE-THRU CRASH
Many companies have jumped on the trend of deploying AI in their business and marketing without thinking it through. McDonald's worked with IBM for three years to leverage AI to take drive-thru orders. It called it off in June 2024. The proof needed wasn't in the data. It was in a raft of videos of the actual customer experience, with people desperately trying to get the AI to understand their order.

Over-complicating the message, the packaging, the instructions, the marketing
You may be in a highly technical business. What's inside or behind your product or your service may be very complicated. Marketing is in the communication business. Your job is to make things as simple as possible, so you don't get in the way of your audience's understanding.

CASE STUDY: THE MAC VS PC CAMPAIGN
Microsoft had a dominant position in PC software but overcomplicated its packaging and product delivery.[28] In the early 2000s, Microsoft had setbacks with its Windows Vista operating system failing in the market. There were running gags about software being launched with ongoing patches. There were security issues with viruses. The *Guardian* summarised the issue as 'Windows Vista fails to do what a good operating system is meant to do: make life simpler'.[29] In 2006, Apple went on the offensive and, over the years that followed, ran sixty-six

commercials in a campaign called 'Mac vs PC'. Two characters, a suit-wearing man representing the PC and the Mac as a man in a T-shirt and jeans, played out jokes at PC's expense on how complicated and unfriendly being a PC customer was. It was a further build on Apple's brand consistency – contrasting its ease of use and approachability against the competition's complexity and remoteness.

Brand-deaf social media engagement

Advertising copywriter David Abbott once said, 'Shit that arrives at the speed of light is still shit.' In the case of brands and their communication in an always-on social media world, this has never been truer. There are five billion people on social media, which is about two-thirds of the world's population. The opportunity for a brand to get it wrong has never been greater. Brands are rushing to have ever more content appear everywhere. That means there are more people in more places who need to get the brand or think more about the audience and the media realities of what they are doing. The opportunities to score an 'own goal' are everywhere.

CASE STUDY: BURGER KING FALLS OFF THE INTERNATIONAL WOMEN'S DAY BANDWAGON

Nowadays, everyone likes to jump on a topic and try to grab attention for the brand. Burger King tweeted on International Women's Day, 'Women belong in the kitchen'. They wanted to show that they had a new scholarship programme for female employees. It came across as an utterly insensitive attention-seeking hijack of International Women's Day. Burger King was forced to apologise and delete the tweet, but the damage was done.

Not checking brand marketing with an audience first

Many brand blunders could have been prevented just by running a product, brand name, slogan or commercial past its potential market and asking, 'Is this OK? Can you imagine any issues?' It would have avoided...

- In 2017, Adidas emailed runners who had just finished the Boston Marathon with the subject line, 'Congrats you survived the Boston Marathon.' In 2013, three people were killed and more than 260 were injured in the Boston Marathon bombing.
- Scandinavian company, Electrolux, had a slogan 'Nothing Sucks Like an Electrolux' for its vacuum cleaners. In the UK, the literal meaning of greater suction was taken out when it ran its marketing. However, in the USA, 'Sucks' had much stronger associations as slang for not working or bad. It left customers confused about whether the brand was being promoted or insulted.

Summary

When you look back at our list of typical reasons for when a brand goes wrong, they aren't marketing technicalities. The common factors are arrogance, complacency, incompetence or laziness. It's almost certain all these mistakes will happen again:

- Living in a marketing jargon land.
- Not understanding your audience's needs or preferences.
- Becoming generic.
- Over-promising and under-delivering.
- Forgetting that consistency is the essence of great brands.
- Losing control of your brand delivery.
- Lack of crisis planning and management.
- Relying solely on data as the answer.
- Over-complicating the brand and its messaging.
- Brand-deaf social media engagement.
- Not checking your brand marketing with an audience first.

10

How to Redraw a Market Map in your Audience's Mind

I wisely started with a map, and made the story fit it.
J.R.R. TOLKIEN, WRITING TO NAOMI MITCHISON IN 1954 ABOUT
WRITING *THE LORD OF THE RINGS*

Marketers often portray the audience decision-making process in their market as linear – as if it was like herding sheep from the mountains into a field and then into a nice, neat pen. The classic model is AIDA: 'awareness', followed by 'interest', then 'desire', then 'action'. In a general sense, it's true; if I'm not aware of you, I'm much less likely to buy from you. However, you can go straight to 'action' via search or comparison sites and 'desire' via social media or partnership.

Stop constraining your brand and market thinking. One of the best ways to get a fresh perspective on your brand and its market is to step away from a linear mindset. Try to think and express your market spatially in how you explore, think and play with questions and draw maps:

- What might your audience think about how the market looks?
- How could your brand be positioned or repositioned on that map?

Perceptual mapping

There is a market map inside your audience's head. On this map, your brand and others you compete against are fighting it out inside your audience's mind to be noticed and chosen. Try to visualise this as a map on which the audience imagines brands positioned against their rivals based on the key factors on which choices in the market are made. Your audiences don't actively think about this map. It's just used subconsciously in a buying situation. However, if you ask them the right questions, observe them or use research, you can redraw it and look to change the map in your brand's favour.

More brands and marketers need to learn how to discover this map and explore what it could be.

Perceptual mapping is a common approach used in consumer focus groups to understand people's perceptions of brands and the market. It's also an approach you can do internally with colleagues or get your distributors to draw their perceptual market maps.

Stage 1: Explain the purpose and concept of perceptual mapping

- Tell the group the objective of the task is to place brands on a map and visually represent how consumers perceive differences between the different brands.
- Show them one or two examples of perceptual maps. You could pick a selection of different food products and explain how you might put them on a map that has descriptors at the axes of, e.g., 'sweet' vs 'savoury' and 'expensive' vs 'affordable'. It's often a good idea to have fun with this and get them into the idea, e.g., how might you map Premier League Football teams in different ways. What you are doing is getting them into perceptual mode.

Stage 2: Collect initial impressions of products/services

- Distribute some products or image stimulus for the products.
- Before getting people to draw the map, get them to say what comes to mind for each product. Capture their answers for each product on a Post-it note.
- Allow them to interact, discuss and share different views.

- Prompt them with questions. For example, if you were creating a perceptual map for vodkas, ask:
  - 'What's your first impression of each product?'
  - 'How would you describe it if you were explaining it to someone else?'
  - 'What stands out about this product that makes it unique or different from most other products?'

Stage 3: Facilitate a discussion about market differentiators

- Encourage people to suggest characteristics that separate the brands when they think about buying them.
- Write the suggestions on a whiteboard.
- Remind them of the perception mapping example of 'sweet' vs 'savoury'. Get them to play a game of suggesting what a variety of opposite axes of the map might be.
- Prompt with some more questions to further identify axes descriptions:
  - 'What makes one brand better, worse or different from another?'
  - 'If you were choosing one for yourself, what factors would influence your decision?'
  - 'What do you think matters most to people when choosing a product like this?'

Step 4: Choose two dimensions for the map

- Having opened things up with options and questions, you now ask the group to choose just two polarities (horizontal and vertical).
- Tell them they need to choose, but 'Don't worry, we can discuss it later and change it'.
- Examples for vodka might be:
  - 'Traditional' vs 'trendy' or 'smooth' vs 'strong' or 'premium' vs 'value'.

- Ask questions to finalise the axes:
  - 'Which of these attributes feels most important in differentiating these products?'
  - 'Are there other opposites that make sense to you in how we could separate the brands in the market?'
  - 'If you had to choose just two dimensions, which ones would you choose to rank these brands most effectively?'

Step 5: Place the brands on the perceptual map

- With the axes defined, people can now put the brands (typically written on Post-it notes) on the map.
- Before anyone puts anything up, ask them to think individually about where they would put them on the map and why. This minimises group thinking and allows for discussion of different views.
- Ask one of them to start by putting the brands on the map based on their agreed-upon criteria.
- Ask others to comment and discuss if they agree or disagree and why. Then, the brands should be moved to what is agreed to be better positions.
  Questions during placement could be:
  - 'Why do you have Brand A here, so close to Brand B?'
  - 'What were the reasons why you placed Brand A here?'
  - 'Does anyone disagree?' Tell them it's OK to disagree and you want different perspectives.

Step 6: Reflect and review

- Once you have a complete map, review it with the group and take notes.
- Make sure you take a photo. Explore any linked insights or thoughts with them. Helpful questions to ask include:
  - 'Does the placement represent your overall feelings about the brands or is something missing?'

- 'Are there any brands we could move or are missing?' As you get an answer to this, also think and probe to find, 'What does this tell you about how people see products differently and make choices when they get to choose? Is there an insight or idea to explore further?

- 'Are there different places or circumstances where this map doesn't apply?' For example, people may choose a more premium vodka when in a bar with friends than they'd buy in a supermarket.

- 'Are there any different maps within this map for certain audiences, products and attitudes (e.g., sustainable fashion as a subset within a fashion)? Are there bigger maps with other products on where the existing product choices might also appear (e.g., are EV automotives just on an automotive map or are they part of a bigger set of environmental behaviours)? Now that we have done this exercise, has anyone got any suggestions for the axes that we might use instead that might change how we see preferences and decisions?'

FACILITATOR'S NOTE

Having done this type of exercise many times, you may notice that some axes come up time and again, such as 'high price' vs 'low price' or 'high quality' vs 'low quality'. This may be the case, but it's best to ask people to think and describe more deeply and less generically. Also, encourage people to think in different dimensions, e.g., impatience, speed, etc.

Exercise: Draw your own market map

Whilst the perceptual mapping approach is excellent to do in a group, you can also do it on your own. It's a great way to challenge your thoughts. Earlier in the book, we discussed the marketing fuss over Jaguar's repositioning. They are likely to have done an equivalent of this and then decided to move Jaguar on their map.

Example: Women's high fashion

You may not be knowledgeable about fashion. However, I can still use it as an example to show perceptual mapping and then walk you through examples of how discussions might then continue.

This map is a simple one I adapted for women's fashion brands. The perceived axes are 'modern' vs 'classic' and 'high class' vs 'high street'. Now we have a draft map drawn for the women's high fashion market, we can probe, discuss and adapt.

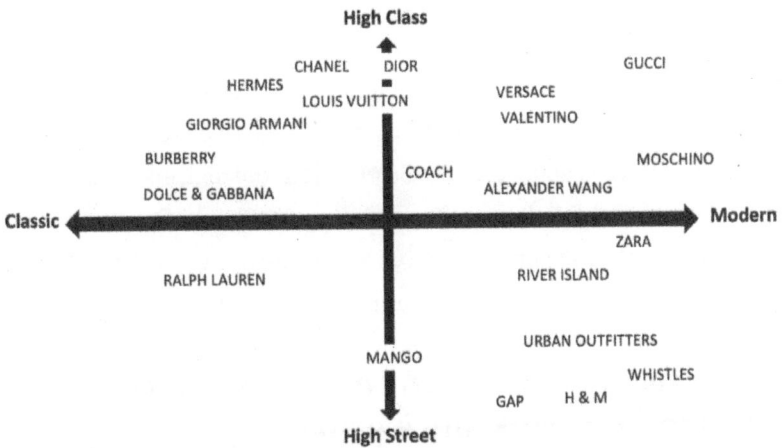

Maps provide the benefit of a prototype

We end up with a prototype because a market map is created by group facilitation rather than presentation. Its axes are the result of discussion too. The great thing about prototypes is that people find them much easier to comment on, change or improve. So, using our women's fashion prototype perceptual map, here are some examples of what insights might come out of a prompted discussion. You may agree or disagree with them. That's fine, as the point is to explore what a map could be:

- We don't have mainstream fashion retailers that offer well-made fashion with value like Marks & Spencer and John Lewis on the map.
- Chanel must be moved further to the left and considered more classic.
- Burberry doesn't fit this map. It has become less luxurious and confused in its brand positioning. You might then ask where it fits or what axes you would use. Imagine you were doing Burberry's brand repositioning.
- It's missing the trend towards sports or rugged chic like Arc'teryx or North Face.
- It doesn't consider the consumers' need for sustainability and not wanting fast fashion with disposable clothes. You probe to explain, and they tell you, Stella McCartney is at the high end of this with her ethical fashion, as is the more mainstream Patagonia. You might ask the person who raised this how they might redraw a different map that includes ethical or sustainable fashion.

Perceptual mapping turns market and brand position from work into a game

Suddenly, exploring your brand positioning is less of a task and more of a game. Now imagine doing this perceptual market mapping game as a way to explore the positioning of:

- Automotive brands for electric vehicles – e.g., BMW, Tesla or Honda.
- Online search, security and tracking – e.g., for DuckDuckGo, Google, NordVPN and Norton.
- B2B marketing automation platforms – e.g., for Salesforce, Adobe, HubSpot, Oracle and Zoho.
- Ways I can get to Paris from London, e.g., British Airways, Eurostar, Eurotunnel, EasyJet, Ryanair.

Carry on playing and carry on learning

Put the term 'perceptual maps of brands in different markets' into Google and press the image filter. You'll soon be able to explore different maps for different markets. You may look at them and think this is done by experts. They may have even been done based on research data. However, it's based on the same process I've just described. So, nothing is stopping you from trying. There isn't a right or wrong.

Repositioning your brand on the perceptual market map

Once you've created some market maps and found out where your brand is perceived on one, you should do something about it.

- Suppose the parameters of the audience map suit your brand. You should reinforce the factors that support it. For example, if customer service matters and you are the best for customer service then own it as a brand and bring the benefits of what makes your customer service different to life.

- Alternatively, if you find your brand in a position on the map you don't want to be in, or just part of a crowd, you shouldn't ignore it. That's where the job of a true marketer starts. You need to look at things in your brand, the market and your story that you can use to change these perceptions.

Below is an illustrative map for the vodka market before Grey Goose enters in the 1990s (see also Chapter 5). People had been brought up to believe the best vodka was Russian. The Swedish brand Absolut with a large marketing spend communicating purity had eventually managed to move itself up in quality perceptions. Simplistically, however, if this was the consumers' perceived market map, then if a vodka wasn't Russian or a brand couldn't spend heavily on things like advertising it would struggle to ever charge a premium.

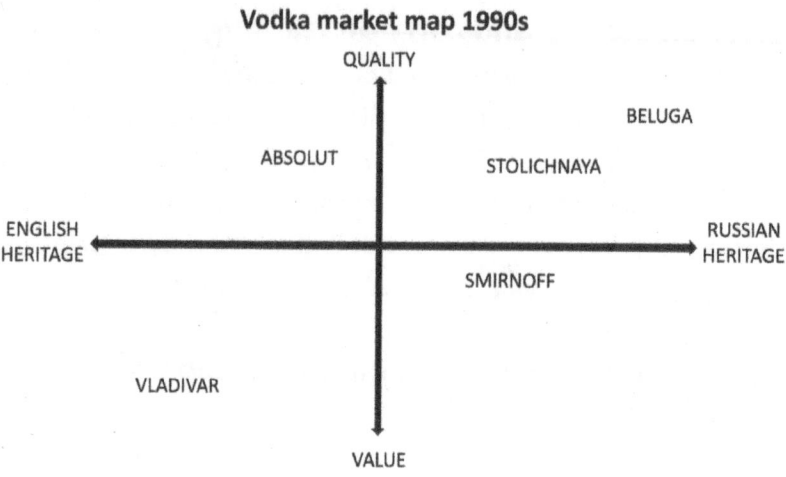

Vodka market map 1990s

Redrawing the market map

Marketing isn't about accepting perceptions the way they are, but looking for insights, ideas and actions that can change things in your brand's favour.

An excellent way to do this is to think of how to redraw the market map. This is what many of the best brands do. If you think of First Direct, Airbnb, Uber, Apple, Grey Goose, Tesla – they all became stand-out brands by redrawing the map.

As you look into a market and the brands in it, always look for:

- What is an unmet need?
- What is a new way to get the audience to consider what matters?
- What changes are happening in society or the market I can tap into?

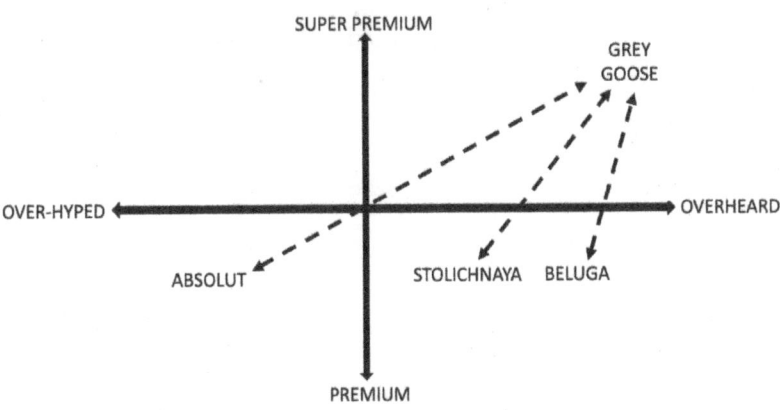

Vodka market Grey Goose re-invented

CASE STUDY: GREY GOOSE

On the earlier (existing market) map, Absolut had accepted how the vodka market map worked inside a consumer's head. They accepted Russian heritage remained the dominant quality association and differentiation. They instead chose to market themselves on purity to move up in quality perceptions. Grey Goose, however, redrew the map. It established itself as the best-tasting vodka and redrew the market in its favour to be in a new category of its own: super-premium. In the process, it didn't just position itself. It redrew the market axes and repositioned where Russian vodka was now perceived to be. It turned the vertical axis to be 'super-premium' vs 'premium'. It completely removed several vodkas from being in the redrawn market. It also changed the horizontal axis to 'over-hyped' vs 'overheard'. This played to the exclusivity it was building in how the brand was promoted, distributed and discovered.

CASE STUDY: APPLE VS PCS

Steve Jobs returned to Apple in 1997. It was a boom time for personal computers. If you had a perceptual market map for the market, it might have looked like this:

Everyone wanted a home or office PC, but PCs were expensive. The more prominent brands traded on trust and charged a premium. There were value brands, which were 'boxes'. The leading challenger brand was Dell. Dell changed the market model and built PCs to order (customers could specify components), delivering them directly rather than via stores. This also meant it was perceived as quality with value. So, in this market map, the horizontal is 'buy more on memory offered' vs 'buy more on brand history', and the vertical axis is 'buy minimum can get away with' vs 'buy the best can afford'.

Steve Jobs and Apple recognised that the reality of the market was all beige boxes that looked the same and had similar components. He also noticed that marketing for many brands was about how much memory they offered and what you got for your money. Apple was about how its particular brand brought the benefit of making your life easier. Jobs and Apple exposed a truth in the market from a user's perspective and then designed and marketed Apple to answer it. It changed the vertical axis to 'aesthetic design' vs 'beige boxes' and the horizontal axis to 'complicated to use' vs 'make life easier'.

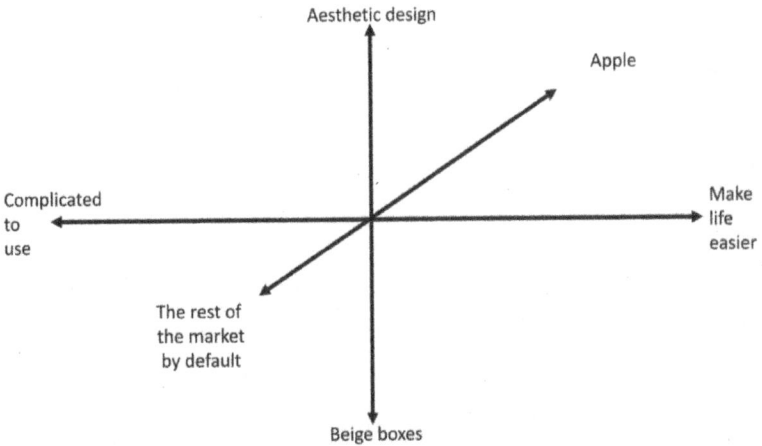

It simplifies what the Apple brand does and they've pretty much carried on in that vein ever since. If ever there is a brand based on redrawing market maps, it is Apple – PCs, phones, music, etc. Steve Jobs once said, 'Some people say give the customers what they want, but that's not my approach. Our job is to figure out what they're going to want before they do.'

Summary
Perceptual market mapping brings fresh perspectives to how a brand might see itself and its market from its audience's perspective. It's remarkably easy to do and turns a vital aspect of developing brand and market positioning into a game you can play individually or in a team.

Because you are spatially exploring the market you operate in, it's easy to develop alternative maps of how a market can be perceived. From there you can reconsider how your brand and its positioning could be made more credible, accessible, relevant and distinctive. In the process, you can take action on three key areas:

1. Ensure your brand is actually on the map for weighing up choices and making decisions in the customer's head. Historically, big banks thought they knew how customers saw banking. They were slow to wake up to the reality that they were now on a map where digital banking, transparency and quality of user experience mattered more. New digital banks took advantage of their thinking to position themselves as challengers and reposition the big banks as the slow establishment.

2. Give your brand the best chance of positioning itself in an area on that map where customers are more likely to buy from you. Major beer brands have historically seen low-alcohol products as necessary versions, with an adequate taste for functional occasions when people couldn't drink. Guinness when creating 0.0 recognised a much larger cultural movement was taking place. They saw the rise of 'NoLo' (no- and low-alcohol) and embraced it. A modern drinker who prioritises wellness without sacrificing taste and experience. They want to be social, don't want to compromise on taste or have to defend themselves from pressure to have a 'real beer'. Guinness 0.0 invested in this insight technologically. It also positioned and communicated 0.0, strengthening the overall brand, celebrating its taste and rituals whilst embracing a more flexible drinking experience, where consumers can choose, or moderate, depending on the occasion without compromise. It's been a huge success, attracting new customers and people who alternate between Guinness 0.0 and regular Guinness (known as Zebras), especially at lunchtimes.

3. Look to change how the map inside your customers' heads is redrawn in your favour. Redraw what matters more on the map, such as where you have or can develop a compelling differentiation against your competition. We've given great examples of how Grey Goose and Apple did just this. Whether an established brand in an established market, or a start-up, the exercise of trying to redraw the market map in your favour is a great way to unclog brand and positioning thinking.

11

Nailing a Value Proposition

When solving problems, dig at the roots instead of just
hacking at the leaves.
ANTHONY J D'ANGELO, AUTHOR

I've been making guest appearances at London Business School (LBS) for a few years. I've run the marketing module on their 'Launchpad' programme. LBS Launchpad is a start-up pre-accelerator programme that brings together some of London's brightest minds to transform ideas into viable businesses.

The concepts I've seen and the people I've met are genuinely inspiring and diverse.

I would speak to the investors who judged the final pitches every year. I asked what was right and what was missing? Why did some get shortlisted and win where others fell by the wayside? I asked these questions to try to understand what they could do better in their marketing. I wasn't looking for how good the business idea was or the calibre and track record of the people, which also clearly matters.

The investors' advice was that if start-ups did only one thing in
marketing to appeal to them, it would be to build a business idea on a more
potent and clearer value proposition.

A good way of thinking of a value proposition is that it explains these two things from your audience's perspective:

1.   How your product solves customers' problems or improves their situation (relevancy).

2.   How it delivers specific benefits (quantified value).

If you get a value proposition right, it's among the most compelling things you can do in marketing.

- For a start-up, it's the thing an investor is looking for more than anything and it's why they should invest.
- For a brand, it's why your audience should choose you on an ongoing basis.
- In a B2B presentation or meeting, it is often your most compelling reason to buy.
- If you have a company website, it's often what you'll explain when people land on it to get them to stay and go further.

A value proposition is simply a statement explaining what the company's service or product does and its benefits. However, getting to a compelling value proposition is something you really need to think about. The best way I can do that is to show you some real examples and get you to figure out the value propositions.

DOLLAR SHAVE CLUB VALUE PROPOSITION

Remember Dollar Shave Club (Chapter 7, p. 77) and how it took on and stood out from Gillette? I'll give you two alternative value propositions they might have used.

A.   A more rational one: 'Dollar Shave Club provides high-quality razors and personal care products at an affordable price, delivered straight to your door.'

B.   A more emotional one: 'Great razors at a great price, simply delivered to your door when you need them, without paying for all the marketing bullsh*t.'

Personally, I'd go with B. It captures and leverages Dollar Shave Club's brand attitude – being the people's champion against a big corporation they imply are over marketing and charging too much for razors.

FRESHBOOKS VALUE PROPOSITION

Big firms have finance departments full of accountants. Smaller businesses have fewer resources but still need to do their accounts, pay taxes and make payroll. People running these businesses also spend time running the business. They may be commercially savvy, but that doesn't make them an accountant.

What's the customer's problem FreshBooks solve?

- Businesspeople either spend more time doing the accounts (which is not their skill), or they have to take money out of the business to hire accountants.
- They want to focus on running their small business, not balancing their books.
- They've tried doing it themselves with existing accountancy packages, but these aren't user-friendly.

What specific benefits does FreshBooks deliver to the customer?

- They offer a software solution designed around a small business owner's reality, not an accountant's.
- It's easy to use, not time-consuming, and delivers a service you need that would usually be handled by accountants.
- You'll be dealing with a company that communicates in a straightforward and approachable manner.

FreshBook's value proposition is: 'Small business accounting software designed for you, the non-accountant.'

DuckDuckGo value proposition

Everybody uses online searches all the time. It's become a default behaviour. Google is the dominant player. There is nothing stopping people from choosing another search engine, but Google has become an ingrained habit. Each time we search via Google, we know we are supplying data about what we do and what we search. Google might tell us this allows it to generate more accurate search answers to match our needs. But many people feel it is creepy to have suggestions pop up via ads you haven't asked for as you go from website to website (you only asked about Viagra once).

DuckDuckGo is a search engine designed to be different. It has zero data collection from you. It doesn't gather any personal data or search history information. Even the users' IP addresses are anonymised. Collecting less data from you also makes DuckDuckGo faster.

Remember, we want benefits, not features. In analysing this, you could argue that there are three territories where DuckDuckGo solves its customer's problems and delivers quantifiable benefits.

1. Speed. It gets to answers quicker.
2. Privacy. You are totally anonymous.
3. Ads won't follow you. It doesn't use your search behaviour to follow you around the internet serving up ads.

This is an example of real-world decisions a brand might need to make to figure out its value proposition. All three of the benefits are true. Each shows why DuckDuckGo is differentiated from the dominant competitor, Google. However, which one do you choose?

In the world of brands and big businesses, this is where you would research all three or combinations of them. You'd find out the most motivating and persuasive way to describe what DuckDuckGo offers to get people to switch from Google. You should research all three areas for different audiences. Younger people may be less bothered about privacy and more bothered by speed. That's something you would want to know and use.

DuckDuckGo based their value proposition around option 2: privacy.

Why I think they did this:

- Speed is not much of an additional benefit. It's not a prime reason to switch. Google doesn't feel that slow.
- Ads won't follow you is a benefit, but this issue is one of annoyance.
- I'm guessing (I haven't researched it) that they've focused on privacy as the lead in their value proposition because it makes people angry when they think about it. From the audience's perspective, privacy is something that Google isn't respecting. Privacy is the most emotive way to connect to audience issues while differentiating DuckDuckGo from its competitors.
- Privacy confirms how and why DuckDuckGo is better – they can fix this problem.

I'd suggest DuckDuckGo's fuller value proposition might be: 'Truly private web browsing that never tracks you.'

Knowing its value proposition then helps it work out how to communicate more powerfully by leading on its primary benefits rather than its features.

If you check out its communication, DuckDuckGo brings the value proposition to life in three steps:

1. It flags an issue its audience will agree with as a question. For example, 'Tired of being tracked online? We can help.'
2. It then answers it.
3. It then shows them the evidence to believe that answer so they can trust DuckDuckGo to fix it.

It gives them an immediate answer to its audience's primary problem to encourage them to try it.

SONY WALKMAN

I'm going back in time to share the value proposition process for one of the most iconic brands and products ever. This time, I want you to create the value proposition yourself by following five steps.

Today, we take it for granted that we can get music wirelessly to our ears. We can ask for any song and it plays. All we have to do is speak – to our smart speaker or AI-powered digital assistant (such as the Siri feature in Apple's iPhone) – and music happens. If we are not sure, something can be recommended. With AI, you can prompt and a song will be created in moments.

There was a time when music was physically recorded and then physically played. It was on vinyl and then on tapes. Sony was a leading manufacturer of equipment that enabled you to listen to music at home. They also sold portable radios and relatively large cassette tape recorders.

Masaru Ibuka, Sony's co-founder, often travelled for business. He would lug Sony's bulky TC-D5 cassette recorder around to listen to music. He asked for one to be designed that was less heavy and functioned just to play music back. This brief created the Sony Walkman. Sony released it in the 1980s. It is difficult to explain the change this caused in society. The 1980s was the Walkman decade. 'Walkman' entered the *Oxford English Dictionary* as a word in 1986.

Now, imagine you are in the marketing department at Sony. You are announcing this idea to the media and consumers. Here are five key questions you can use to help discover a value proposition. I've filled them out for the Sony Walkman to help explain. What would you say is the Sony Walkman's value proposition?

1. What are the benefits your product/service offers? (Remember we're looking for benefits, not features.)

- It's lighter.
- It's more portable.
- It makes it easier to listen to music as you travel/move.

2. Describe what makes these benefits valuable.
- You don't have to carry around something heavy to listen to music.
- The headphones mean it allows you to listen to your music without disturbing others.
- You can cycle, skateboard and run while listening to music.
- You can choose your own music to listen to and don't have to listen to what may be playing in a store or on the radio.
- It's a new technology that feels cool to own and for people to see you using.

3. What are the customer's main problems?
- They can't just listen to music wherever they are and whatever they are doing.
- Outside of their own room, they can't decide what they listen to.
- Travelling between places or exercising may be good for them, but it's dull to do.
- It's a physical chore if they want to take their music from their home to anywhere else.

4. How can you connect the benefits you offer to your potential buyer's problems?
- They can listen to music outside without it hurting their back.
- Wherever they are, they get to choose what music they listen to.
- The music they own is liberated from their home.

5. How would you differentiate yourself from the competition as the preferred provider of this value?

- This is a new technology innovation – a first. We can decide what it is called and own the name.
- Sony's worldwide reputation as a pioneer in new technology – from radio to cassettes to TV. Sony created the first truly portable radio, the smallest radio and the first truly portable TV.
- The name Sony comes from Sonus, the Latin word meaning sound.
- Japan was seen as a leading country in technology, and Sony was the leading company from Japan.
- There was nothing like it that you could buy as an alternative.
- Though portable radios already existed, this was the only portable device that allowed people to choose their music.
- Headphones existed, but they were big and heavy. The device was being introduced with new, light, portable headphones with high-quality sound reproduction.

How did you get on, figuring out the Sony Walkman value proposition?

Just like any new Apple product benefits today in that it comes from Apple, at the time, Sony had incredible traits in its brand that differentiated it from competitive brands. It provided brand protection when other brands followed and copied. Specifically:

- It had a track record of innovation.
- It was the best of the best as a technology company from Japan.
- It was known for exceptional audio.
- Sony as a brand was prestigious and cool.

Following through this five-step process, I'd suggest a Sony Walkman value proposition might be: 'A personal music revolution – choose and listen to your music as you move.'

Here's how I arrived at this value proposition:

- Portable is true, but *'as you move'* is better. It has more energy and dynamism linked to what you're doing rather than just carrying.
- You have to add the ability to *'choose and listen'*. It shows the difference of the Sony Walkman to portable radio. Liberating and controlling your music choice is a huge benefit and difference.
- To tap into the Sony brand reputation for innovation and that this is a first, I've added *'a personal music revolution'*.

If you followed a feature-led approach, you could have described it as lighter, portable, for travel, etc. Interestingly, the product started off being called different names in different countries. It might have been called the Soundabout, the Stowaway or the Freestyle. You can see where feature-led value propositions could have influenced those names. Ultimately, a vital part of the Sony brand protection was owning the first and ultimate device by combining the brand and product name to be Sony Walkman.

How a value proposition differs from a brand positioning

Value proposition and brand positioning are two other marketing terms that get conflated. They are linked but they are different.

- Your 'value proposition' helps show your audience or sales prospect how they can solve a problem. The value proposition helps them imagine your solution and the benefits they'll get as a result. The value proposition for the Apple iPhone might be 'a powerful, intuitive smartphone that connects your life seamlessly'.
- Your 'brand positioning statement' allows you to spell out why *your* solution is preferable and *why it stands out against competitive alternatives.* The brand positioning for the Apple iPhone might therefore be instead 'the premium, innovative smartphone for those who think differently'.

The simplest way to explain brand positioning is to depict it as three overlapping circles.

- A winning positioning is where your brand offers something the audience wants, and which your competitor doesn't offer.
- A dumb positioning is offering something your competitors offer, and which your customers don't want.
- A losing positioning is your competitor offering something the audience want, and which your brand doesn't offer.

In a Tesla vs BMW electric vehicle buying scenario:

- Tesla may emphasise greater driving range or availability of chargers – pushing a specific point of difference.
- BMW might make the point that more and more people in Europe try both vehicles and choose a BMW.

Here's an example of what might be Amazon's brand positioning statement:

'For consumers who want to purchase a wide range of products online with quick delivery, Amazon is a one-stop online shopping site. Amazon sets itself apart from other online retailers with its customer obsession, passion for innovation and commitment to operational excellence.'

Summary

Investors in start-ups view having a strong and compelling value proposition as a crucial reason to invest. A value proposition is simply a statement explaining what the company's service or product does and its benefits. However, getting to a compelling value proposition is something you need to think about.

A good way of thinking of a value proposition is that it explains these two things from your audience's perspective:

- How your product solves customers' problems or improves their situation (relevancy).
- How it delivers specific benefits (quantified value).

Value proposition and brand positioning are marketing terms that get conflated.

- Your 'value proposition' helps show your audience or sales prospect how they can solve a problem.
- Your 'brand positioning statement' allows you to spell out why your solution is preferable and why it stands out against competitive alternatives.

12

Build Your Own Brand Key

A very little key will open a very heavy door.
CHARLES DICKENS, HUNTED DOWN, 1859

There are lots of processes around marketing that help a business understand and communicate its brand's core message, values and positioning. The 'Brand Key' approach was created by Unilever, one of the world's largest and most successful consumer goods companies.

In my view, the Brand Key is one of the most accessible and useful approaches to work with any business and team. You don't need to be a marketer to use it. It can help shape the strategic direction of side hustles, start-ups and large corporations. You can also use it as a framework for a core team to work through a brand or product in a workshop.

To show how applicable it is for brands and marketing, I've populated one for the Sony Walkman, which we looked at in the last chapter. The Sony Walkman was launched twenty years before the Brand Key's invention. The Brand Key as an approach survives the test of time.

Just read the key below. Does it help you get the strategic approach that led to the positioning of the Sony Walkman brand? You can use the same approach for the brand and product you are working on today.

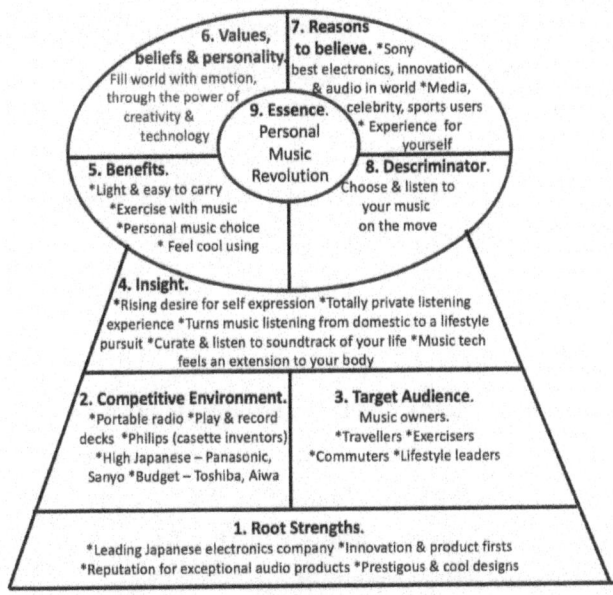

A Brand Key is a step-by-step process that describes what a brand is all about, boiling down its essence into a few words. To make the Brand Key accessible, I've converted it into a questionnaire (below). The questionnaire is one of the things I'll send in advance when meeting a start-up or a new client. I'll ask them to think about their answers in advance of our first meeting.

Read the questionnaire. Before doing so, have in mind a real brand or challenge you want to build a Brand Key for. It could be your current business, your competitor, a start-up idea or another brand example.

Use it as a lens when you look at other businesses and brands. Remember to:

- Really understand your consumers'/customers' wants and needs.
- Define and build your own brand story – not a generic one.

Don't worry about finding the perfect words or sentences. It's more important that you put down what comes to mind. If you struggle in an area, it will point to something you might need to work on to make your business idea clearer or more compelling.

This part is **important**. Your job with the questionnaire is to get as much information and as many insights and ideas as possible in each area. In the Sony Walkman example, I've condensed it, having done a fuller process. At this stage, the job is not to reduce your thinking, so it fits into the physical key. You can do that much later.

Questionnaire

1. **Root strengths:** What are the brand foundations we can build on – the primary or original attributes/values/ benefits of your business idea, its history or its founders? If it's a start-up or a new idea, what is the evidence you have that this is a market opportunity?

2. **Competitive environment:** What brands compete with your current brand or your new idea? What are the alternative choices seen by the consumer/user? What is the relative value of your brand as seen by the consumer/user as we know it?

3. **Target audience:** How would you describe the people and situations for which your brand is always the best choice? How would you define the target audience, including their attitudes and values – as well as the number and type of customer?

4. **Insight:** What insights do we have into the market or the business? Insights tell all that you know about how the market works or fails now. When finding insights you are looking from the perspective of the target audience and their needs, latent needs, purchase motives and the opportunities for the business in the market. Don't simply write down information. Insight is finding something that helps you understand the situation or problem differently. What makes you go, 'That's interesting and makes me think'?

5. **Benefits:** What are the functional, emotional or other benefits you offer against alternatives that motivate your audience to buy your brand? A functional benefit might be based on a

product/service attribute that provides utility to your audience. An emotional benefit gives richness, feelings and depth to the experience of using your brand. Understanding the difference between detailing a product/service 'feature' and converting it to an audience 'benefit' matters. You can write down features, but you must turn them into benefits.

6. **Values, beliefs and personality**: What are the values that the brand stands for and believes in? What is the personality of the brand, or what would you like it to be? If your brand were a person, or a fictional character, or a movie, or a book, what would it be? What other brands or businesses do you admire that capture how you would like your company to behave? What behaviours would your company always do/never do?

7. **Reasons to believe:** Why do you believe that what you offer is better or different than the alternative? How would you describe, in the customer's voice, the reasons they can believe that the promises and the brand's positioning will hold true, come what may? What is the proof that the brand delivers the benefits it claims? What is your case that your brand is the best option for your audience? How would you fill in this sentence from your audience's perspective: 'I buy your brand because ...'?

8. **Discriminator:** Try to find and articulate what is the single most compelling reason for your target audience to choose your brand. How would you describe your brand in one sentence that defines your brand's competitive edge or value proposition? How would you fill in this sentence from your audience's perspective: 'Only your brand has/will ...'?

9. **Essence:** What is the core of your brand, i.e., the brand's essence? It is the one clear thought that describes the brand. What is your brand's genetic code in a clear, simple one-, two- or three-word thought? In the case of BMW, it would be 'driving'. For the Sony Walkman, we arrived at 'personal music revolution'.

Summary

Unilever created the Brand Key approach. It is an easy and helpful approach to brand marketing because it provides a structured yet flexible framework for defining and strengthening a brand's identity. All you have to do is answer the questions in the nine steps. It's a clear structure that builds a holistic brand strategy and story. It's consumer-centric and seeks meaningful insights. It seeks differentiation and stand-out from the competition. It helps guide subsequent key marketing decisions to align communication, innovation and positioning.

13

Let's Go Marketing

Experience is simply the name we give our mistakes.
OSCAR WILDE, *THE PICTURE OF DORIAN GRAY*, 1890

For whatever reason, you bought this book. I thank you. I've been meaning to write it for ages.

I thought I knew a bit about marketing. However, researching it, coming up with what I hope are helpful explanations, examples, stories and conversations with many industry friends, has taught me even more. For example, the fifth P, partnership, wasn't in my head before writing. However, in truth, it's what great marketers do.

As you finish reading this little 'cookbook', I want to leave you with a summary of my thoughts – the takeaway meal, if you like.

Marketing is more art than science. Use the data and the insight but paint pictures, draw maps and create keys. Talk to people, meet people, work with people, get out of your department and get inside your audience's head.

Beware the 'birthday cats' of terminology, general marketing confusion and bullsh*t. Do have opinions, but ask, listen, understand and share. Be more LEGO; marketing needs more 'explorers' than 'exploiters'.

This is meant to be a cookbook, not a TV instruction manual. There isn't a playbook for how you do marketing; you have to figure it out and work out what you want to cook and for whom. The secret ingredient to becoming a better marketing cook is asking better questions. I've taken that approach when I set out to explain things. I hope you can use those questions in all sorts of circumstances. I also hope you develop your own for whatever you are marketing.

In my marketing recipe, we have 5Ps: product, price, promotion, place and partnership. They work together, and they affect each other. Marketing isn't advertising or sales, but they are an essential part of it. Marketing is about getting into your audience's head and finding ways to meet and satisfy their unmet needs with what you create and serve up to them. Remember, a great salesperson can sell ice cream to Inuits. A marketer's job is to make sure they don't have to.

It's easy to launch or sell a product or service. Building brands is much harder, but the challenges and rewards are much greater. The most potent brands have glue and grip. A value proposition or a brand positioning does not mean anything if it's just a document. You need to make it real and multi-dimensional and give it momentum with a clear sense of direction.

A brand is not the logo, the straplines, the looks, the packaging or the ads. Don't let your brand become wrapping paper. Work hard to lift and separate your brand from its competitors. Don't just accept the market as it is; create a space within it so your audience starts questioning why they ever bought your competitors. Think how you could redraw it in your favour.

Get your brand right, make it '360 degree' and write down what it is on a page so that when you need to engage or work with others, they know what they're working with (and that they're working with a pro).

Hindsight is one of marketing's great gifts. You can look at what others have done and learn the good lessons and the bad. Remember, even the most famous and apparently impregnable brands can get lost before they realise it in the marketing and business jungle. That's why your mission, vision and values matter: to keep everybody motivated and moving in the same direction. However busy you are, attentively mind the gap between what you say and what you do. If you spot a gap, don't put off fixing it.

Don't be scared of the numbers. Embrace them. Be in the research groups, chat with the data analysts, apply AI, test and learn. It's great to aspire to get the click-through rate up to 0.0399 per cent, but don't allow what marketing is and how it can work to get siloed. The investors for a start-up or a well-established private limited company are looking for things that affect the bigger picture. That's why adopting a mindset of INSIGHTS>IDEAS>ACTIONS matters. The total business numbers determine how the brand and performance work in the long term. Remember, 'strength of brand/marketing' remains the most frequently cited important factor by analysts (79 per cent).

Consistency is the essence of great brands. One of the things about the most consistent brands that stay the course is that they are not complacent. They don't expect the market, their competitors or their audience to remain static. Some of them force change and others adapt to change quicker, but they stay true to themselves as they've done the hard part of marketing and figured it out.

If you ever get stuck on an idea or question – don't forget you can always steal something and seek inspiration from what others have done (as long as you respect brand trademarks and copyrights). My fallback marketing strategy for the future is to ask, 'What would Ryan Reynolds do?'

I'm hoping there is something to steal from the pages of this book, and you'll enjoy what it helps you cook.

I'll leave you with two final quotations as you learn and do more with marketing. They are from ice hockey legend Wayne Gretzky:

'A good hockey player plays where the puck is. A great hockey player plays where the puck is going to be.'

'You miss 100 per cent of the shots you don't take.'

Endnotes

Introduction

[1] Institute of Practitioners in Advertising and the company Brand Finance 2023, *Marketing Week*, 10 October 2023; 'Brand investment matters to the City, reveals new IPA/Brand Finance Survey', IPA, 10 October 2023, https://ipa.co.uk/news/investment-analystsurvey#:~:text=The%20new%20IPA%2FBrand%20Finance,asked%20how%20they%20appraise%20and

[2] Charlotte Rogers, 'Salary survey 2019: The majority of marketers don't have a marketing qualification' in *Marketing Week*, 9 January 2019, https://www.marketingweek.com/salary-survey-2019-routes-into-marketing/

[3] Kim Bhasin and Lily Meier, 'The Man Who Made Nike Uncool' in Business Week Online, Bloomberg UK, 13 September 2024 https://www.bloomberg.com/news/features/2024-09-13/nike-nke-stock-upheaval-defines-ceo-john-donahoe-s-tenure?embedded-checkout=true

Chapter 1: What Marketing Is and What it Isn't

[4] Seth Godin, *This Is Marketing: You Can't Be Seen Until You Learn to See* (London: Portfolio Penguin, 2018)

[5] Philip Kotler, *Marketing Management* (London: Pearson, 2014)

[6] 'Employees who feel aligned with company values are more likely to stay', Qualtrics.com, 25 April 2022, https://www.qualtrics.com/blog/company-values-employee-retention

Chapter 2: Who, Why, What and Where is Your Audience?

[7] Norman Katkov, *The Fabulous Fanny: The Story of Fanny Brice* (New York: Knopf, 1952)

Chapter 4: What is a Brand?

[8] Geoff Colvin, 'The simple metric that's taking over big business' in *Fortune*, 18 May 2020, https://fortune.com/longform/net-promoter-score-fortune-500-customer-satisfaction-metric/#

Chapter 5: Understanding the 4Ps of Your Marketing Mix

[9] Competition and Markets Authority, 'CMA launches investigation into Ticketmaster over Oasis concert sales', GOV UK online, 5 September 2024, https://www.gov.uk/government/news/cma-launches-investigation-into-ticketmaster-over-oasis-concert-sales; US Office of Public Affairs, 'Justice Department Sues Live Nation-Ticketmaster for Monopolizing Markets

Across the Live Concert Industry', U.S. Department of Justice website, 23 May 2024, https://www.justice.gov/archives/opa/pr/justice-department-sues-live-nation-ticketmaster-monopolizing-markets-across-live-concert

[10] Meaghan Yuen, 'Walmart beat Amazon in worldwide digital ad revenue growth for the second quarter in the past year', *EMARKETER*, 4 September 2024, https://www.emarketer.com/content/walmart-amazon-worldwide-igital-ad-revenue-growth

Chapter 6: Making More of the Fifth P – Partnerships

[11] Tayn Pedler, 'Yeezy come, Yeezy go! Adidas reports first financial loss for many years as a result of ending its deal with Kanye West – losing €75million in 2023 after a €612m profit the year before', *Daily Mail*, 13 March 2024, https://www.dailymail.co.uk/news/article-13192829/adidas-report-financial-loss-75million-euros-2023-kanye-west-deal-ending-result.html; Faarea Masud, 'Adidas ends 'fight' with Kanye West over antisemitism', BBC News online, 29 October 2024, https://www.bbc.co.uk/news/articles/cgej945wp9xo#:~:text=Adidas%20has%20ended%20its%20%22fight,Yeezy%20stock%20at%20wholesale%20prices

Chapter 7: Removing the Confusion Between Purpose, Mission and Vision

[12] What is diversity, equity, and inclusion? 17 August 2022, https://www.mckinsey.com/featured-insights/mckinsey-explainers/what-is-diversity-equity-and-inclusion

[13] Chris Osuh and Joanna Partridge, Rollback on diversity policies 'risks undoing decades of progress', says Co-op, *Guardian*, 14 February 2025, https://www.theguardian.com/business/2025/feb/14/ditching-diversity-risks-progress-co-op

Chapter 8: Values Matter, but Mind the Gap

[14] 'Boeing's Starliner returns to Earth – leaving crew behind' in *Aljazeera*, 7 September 2024, https://www.aljazeera.com/news/2024/9/7/boeings-starliner-returns-to-earth-leaving-crew-behind

[15] Alex Lawson and Callum Jones, 'Boeing will plead guilty to criminal fraud over 737 Max crashes' in the *Guardian*, 8 July 2024, https://www.theguardian.com/business/article/2024/jul/08/boeing-737-max-crashes-guilty-plea-indonesia-ethiopia#:~:text=Boeing%20has%20agreed%20to%20plead,case%20to%20go%20to%20trial.

[16] Donald Sull, Stefano Turconi and Charles Sull, 'When It Comes to Culture, Does Your Company Walk the Talk?', *MIT Sloan Review* online, 21 July 2020, https://sloanreview.mit.edu/article/when-it-comes-to-culture-does-your-company-walk-the-talk

[17] 'About the Culture 500', *MIT Sloan Management Review* online, https://sloanreview.mit.edu/culture500/research

Chapter 9: When Brands Go Wrong

[18] Dave Dye, 'Don't Be Ashamed to S***!' in *Stuff from the Loft*, 9 January 2019, https://davedye.com/2019/01/09/dont-be-ashamed-to-s/

[19] 'H&M apologises over 'racist' image of black boy in hoodie', BBC News online, 8 January 2018, https://www.bbc.co.uk/news/newsbeat-42603960

[20] Dhani Mau, 'H&M group under fire for yet another racist product description' in *Fashionista*, 6 August 2020, https://fashionista.com/2020/08/hm-and-other-stories-racial-slur-beanie

[21] 'Exposed: The Hermes delivery staff throwing your parcels against the wall', *The Times*, 17 December 2021, https://www.thetimes.com/article/exposed-the-hermes-delivery-staff-throwing-your-parcels-against-the-wall-bfkcpnrc3 [RS: CAN'T SEE THIS AS UNDER A PAYWALL]

[22] Liam O'Dell, 'Hermes has rebranded to "Evri" and everyone made the same joke', *Indy100*, 11 October 2022, https://www.indy100.com/news/hermes-evri-meaning-delivery-name-2658423378

[23] Angela Chan, 'Hoover's flight fiasco recalled', BBC News online, 13 May 2004, http://news.bbc.co.uk/1/hi/business/3704669.stm; Jonathan Wells, 'Just what is a Royal Warrant worth?' in *Gentleman's Journal*, 30 April 2025, https://www.thegentlemansjournal.com/article/just-what-is-a-royal-warrant-worth/

[24] Joe Miller, 'What went wrong at Jamie's Italian?', BBC News online, 22 May 2019, https://www.bbc.co.uk/news/business-48355861

[25] 'United Airlines boss sorry for "horrific" passenger removal', BBC News online, 12 April 2017, https://www.bbc.co.uk/news/world-us-canada-39572841#:~:text=Earlier%2C%20Mr%20Munoz%20had%20defended,the%20flight%22%2C%20he%20added

[26] Lucinda Shen, 'United Airlines Stock Drops $1.4 Billion After Passenger-Removal Controversy', *Fortune*, 11 April 2017, https://finance.yahoo.com/news/united-airlines-stock-drops-1-180059108.html

[27] Alexandra Peers, 'Equifax issued wrong credit scores for millions of consumers', CNN Business website, 3 August 2022, https://edition.cnn.com/2022/08/03/business/equifax-wrong-credit-scores/index.html

[28] Jason Hiner, 'The top five reasons why Windows Vista failed' in *ZDNET*, 5 October 2008, https://www.zdnet.com/article/the-top-five-reasons-why-windows-vista-failed/#google_vignette

[29] Charles Arthur, 'Windows Vista: The Smell of Death' *Guardian*, 29 August 2008, https://www.theguardian.com/technology/2008/aug/29/windows.vista

Glossary

In this book, I have tried to demystify and make accessible many of the key aspects of marketing terminology. Marketing as a discipline also often uses terms that are not exactly the same as when used colloquially. In this book various phrases, references and examples used have marketing connotations. I thought it might be helpful to add further context or explanation. I've attempted to do this in the glossary below.

ADVERTISING: In simple marketing terms, advertising is where a company pays to place its messaging or branding in a particular location to expose it to an audience. Consumers, however, often use the term 'advertising' more loosely, and it's worth checking they don't mean branding, packaging, PR, etc.

AI (ARTIFICIAL INTELLIGENCE): A technology that enables computers and machines to use data to simulate human learning, comprehension, problem-solving, decision-making, creativity and even autonomy.

ATTRACTING PROSPECTS: Prospecting is the activity of identifying and contacting potential customers who may be interested in a product or service in order to generate new revenue in the future. You'll often hear terms like 'sales funnel' or 'pipeline'.

AUDIENCE: In marketing terms, the audience is the group of people most likely to be interested in a product or service. Therefore, marketing efforts should typically target this group to achieve a more effective commercial return.

AUDIENCE DECISION PROCESS: The stages a consumer goes through when considering a purchase, from recognising a need to evaluating the purchase afterwards, e.g., problem recognition, information search, alternatives evaluation, purchase decision and post-purchase decision.

AWARENESS: Brand awareness is the extent to which customers can recall or recognise a brand under different conditions. It is a fundamental first step in any marketing.

B2B: Business to business. A company that markets and sells to other businesses as an audience rather than to an end consumer.

B2B2C: Business to business to consumer. A business model where two companies work together to deliver complementary goods or services to the same end customer. For example, a manufacturer produces the product or service, while another business (such as a retailer or marketplace) sells or facilitates the transaction.

B2C: Business to consumer. A company that markets and sells products aimed at end consumers as the target audience.

BIG DATA vs RICH DATA: Big data is characterised by its volume and its velocity: it's vast in size and it's generated rapidly. Rich data is characterised by its quality, depth and context. It provides various perspectives that can often be deployed for marketing in real time. This may include demographics, behaviour, purchase history, communication preferences, social media usage, lifestyle, psychographics, customer journey stage, advertising exposure, previous feedback and reviews, etc. This can all be deployed to inform and execute marketing solutions.

'BOTTOM-UP' MARKETING: This type of marketing strategy is often used by small businesses or start-ups that lack brand recognition. In a bottom-up marketing strategy, the company seeks out customers and then develops products or services to meet their needs.

BOX-TICKING: In marketing, box-ticking means meeting minimum requirements or fulfilling arbitrary tasks, often to the detriment of actual business goals or meaningful brand engagement.

BRAND ASSOCIATIONS: Consumers' mental connections, feelings and responses when they think about a brand.

BRAND DISAPPOINTMENT: The negative emotional state a consumer experiences when a brand's performance, products or services fail to meet their expectations. This leads to dissatisfaction, potentially impacting their brand loyalty and future buying behaviour.

BRAND EXPERIENCE: How the user feels when engaging or interacting with a brand. It's the sum of all sensations, thoughts, feelings and reactions individuals have in response to a brand.

BRAND ICONOGRAPHY: A brand's visual system often goes beyond its logo. Brand iconography is a language of symbols, images and objects used to represent a brand and its core identity.

BRAND PERSONALITY: A set of human traits that define a brand. It's the human characteristics, emotions and attributes consumers associate with a brand.

BRAND SALIENCY: The extent to which a brand is thought of or comes to mind when consumers are making a purchase decision.

BRAND VALUATION: Typically conducted before a business is sold, this process assigns a monetary value to a brand's tangible and intangible assets. Various methodologies are used to assess a brand's contribution (e.g., Apple) to a business's value. One example of a leading company that does brand valuations is Brand Finance.

BREAKFAST TV: TV typically between 5 a.m. and 10 a.m. is when people are getting ready for work or school and might watch TV. It has become a segment in advertiser plans that can be regarded as highly targeted and cost efficient at reaching certain audiences.

CAMPAIGN: A strategic sequence of steps and activities a business takes to reach its audiences and inspire them to purchase products and services or connect with its brands.

CANNIBALISING PROFITS: Introducing a new product that reduces sales volume, revenue or market share of existing products from the same company.

CHALLENGER BRAND: A company or product that actively disrupts the industry status quo or norms, often smaller but with a strong, defiant attitude.

CHANNELS: The medium through which a brand reaches its customers. Examples include stores, digital platforms, social media, TV ads and email.

CHARITY MARKETING: Charities also spend on marketing. They typically do this to gain donations or elicit support, and they need to get an effective return on their marketing spending.

THE CLOUD: Remote servers accessed via the internet that store data and applications, enabling flexible and scalable computing. This has made the cost and speed of using data much cheaper, faster and more accessible for more businesses.

CMS: Content management system. A platform that helps users create, manage and modify website content without understanding computer code.

CONTENT CREATORS: People who create entertaining or educational material in different media, such as social media, TV shows, magazines, newsletters, podcasts, etc.

CONVERTING TO CUSTOMERS: Any business tries to guide a prospect audience from being unaware or a passive observer of a product or service through a journey without losing them to rivals or continuing not to act. 'Converting to customers' is the process of persuading potential customers to take a desired action, leading to them becoming actual customers. Ideally, they want to convert to customers who buy more than once and are positive about the brand.

CORPORATE GOVERNANCE: Rules and systems that ensure transparency, accountability and trust within a company, typically overseen by the board of directors.

COST EFFECTIVE: How return on marketing spend can be evaluated using different metrics. The marketing metrics businesses use don't always tell the real cause and effect of what led to business growth or revenue. This is especially the case where different factors combine in a marketing solution. An evaluation of a form of marketing may appear cost efficient vs a defined metric, but it might not be as cost effective in contributing to bigger business metrics.

COST EFFICIENT: Spending on any form of marketing involves choices and normally involves evaluating the most cost-efficient way to spend money to achieve objectives.

CPC: Cost per click. A revenue model where online publishers charge advertisers every time a user clicks on an ad.

CREATIVITY: Creativity in marketing is different than in art. It's about using unique and inventive approaches to communicate a product or service, or solve a marketing problem. It involves original concepts, designs and storytelling to stand out from the competition and connect to the brand idea.

CRITICAL THINKING: Actively questioning and analysing facts, evidence and arguments to form sound conclusions or decisions.

CRM: Customer relationship management. A system a business uses for managing interactions with past, current and potential customers.

CROWD SOURCED: A marketing strategy involving gathering ideas and input from the public to shape product development or advertising.

CTA: Call to action. A prompt designed to encourage a specific user action, such as clicking a link, making a purchase or signing up for a newsletter.

CTV: Connected TV. Devices that connect to the internet and allow users to stream videos and music or browse the web. TV is no longer just watched in a living room, but on mobiles, laptops, via YouTube, etc.

CUSTOMER EXPERIENCE: How consumers feel about a business throughout their journey, from first awareness to post-purchase.

CUSTOMER JOURNEY: The path a customer takes from awareness to loyalty when interacting with a company. It includes all interactions across various channels and touchpoints, including online, in-store, social media and customer service.

CUSTOMER PROFILE: A customer profile is a document or data profile containing key information about your ideal customer. It would include customer interests, buying patterns, demographics, motivations, pain points and more. The profile can then be used as a guide to creating personalised experiences or brand ideas.

CUSTOMER SERVICE: The assistance and support provided to customers before, during and after a purchase.

CUSTOMER SUPPORT INTERACTIONS: Any communication or engagement between a business and its customers. Typically, these occur when customers are seeking help or assistance with a product or service. Customer support interactions can dramatically affect a brand's reputation. Because of the cost involved in offering customer support using trained humans, customer support has migrated to overseas call centres, then chat, and now AI chatbots. AI doesn't mean that it is worse at delivering customer support than humans, but there is growing frustration among some customers that an ability to get help or resolution to an issue is being passed back to the customer as their problem. This has seen the rise of a new term – enshittification (see entry below).

DATABASE: A structured set of data held in a computer or server that is accessible in various ways. It contains key information on business, audience and marketing that can be analysed and utilised in marketing activity.

DATA SCIENCE: Data science is an indispensable aspect of modern marketing. It is an interdisciplinary field commonly deployed in marketing that combines statistical analysis, machine learning (algorithm-based decisions often using AI) and computer science to extract insights from structured and unstructured data. Marketers can use it to identify markets for products, audiences and behaviours to serve advertising and create real-time messages or offers to maximise product availability or specific audience needs due to interest or circumstance.

DIGITAL AGE: Digital age is a general term often lazily used to justify how marketing has changed. It's characterised by how the widespread use of digital technologies, primarily the internet, mobile devices and social media, has led to a shift from traditional marketing methods to leveraging online/mobile channels and data to connect with customers and drive business outcomes.

DISTRIBUTION CHANNELS: This is covered in more detail under 'place' in Chapter 5 on the 4Ps. It is the path a product or service takes from the producer to the end consumer, including all intermediaries involved. It can be a network of businesses, individuals or systems (especially in an online world) that facilitates discovery, fulfilment and delivery. Many companies will have different distribution channels, e.g., buy directly online or via a store that buys from a wholesaler. Different distribution channels will have different benefits, weaknesses and costs.

ENGAGE WITH CUSTOMERS: Many businesses are looking to sell more than just a product or service. They are actively looking to create ways to interact with customers to build relationships, foster loyalty and encourage repeat business. Greater customer engagement might be achieved through seeking feedback, social media, email marketing, customer service, loyalty programs, customer events, special offers, etc.

ENSHITTIFICATION: A term coined by Cory Doctorow in 2022. The gradual deterioration of a service/product, especially online, due to profit-driven reduction in quality.

EV AUTOMOTIVES: Electric vehicles, as opposed to traditional petrol combustion engine vehicles.

THE 4Ps: Covered in detail in Chapter 5. The 4Ps are a framework for thinking of key elements of product, place, price and promotion that need to be evaluated in building a brand's marketing solution.

GAIN A PRESENCE: A customer can often choose from a myriad of products or services in a market. Gaining a presence typically involves building awareness, creating a positive reputation and engaging with the target audience so that the brand becomes visible and recognisable in a specific market or online space.

GAP IN VALUES: When a company's claimed values contradict its actual behaviour or how it is revealed to be when measured internally or externally.

GENERATIVE AI: A subset of artificial intelligence that focuses on creating new content –such as text, images, video or music – based on learned patterns from existing data.

GEN Z: People born roughly between 1997 and 2012, known as digital natives due to growing up with the internet and smartphones. Gen Z is preceded by Millennials born between 1981 and 1996. It is followed by Generation Alpha born between 2013 and 2024. Whether such large groups' attitudes and behaviours can be homogenised is debatable. However, Gen Z and other groups are frequently referenced in media, business and marketing considerations.

GEO-TARGETED: The ability to target audiences based on geographic location, especially via digital channels.

GLASS DOOR: A website where current and former employees anonymously review companies.

GREENWASHING: The deceptive practice of presenting a company as more environmentally friendly than the reality.

HUBSPOT: A cloud-based CRM platform offering tools to capture and convert business leads, automate processes and manage customer interactions.

IMMEDIATE RETURNS: Marketing campaigns that prioritise and look to evaluate the delivery of measurable results within a quick timeframe, such as a single campaign or a quarter. Typically, this might be ad spend vs sales generated or data captured.

INFLUENCER: A person with a strong following on social media who can influence buying decisions and brand opinions.

INSURANCE AGGREGATOR: A price comparison platform for insurance and other services that allows users to compare and book more easily through one interface.

JOINED-UP SOLUTION: Marketing and brands are not just one aspect, like advertising, packaging, product or sales. Brands are the sum of their parts and how the different elements of marketing 'join-up' to create a more integrated experience.

LOGO: A visual mark representing a brand, often the first thing customers associate with a company.

MACHINE LEARNING ALGORITHMS: Systems that analyse data, find patterns and predict outcomes to enhance targeting and understand consumer behaviour.

MANAGEMENT CONSULTANT: Companies like McKinsey or Deloitte offer professional advice about how to run a company or organisation more effectively. They tend to focus on internal operations, organisational performance and strategic planning. A marketing consultant, by comparison, focuses more on external factors like the brand, customer engagement, market research and helping businesses connect what they do via marketing strategies to positively affect sales to their audience.

MARKET: Market is one of those terms used in different ways by different people in marketing. Market can mean the total audience available to buy your product or service, e.g. the car market. Market can mean the more specific potential audience or segment (the pool of buyers) to buy your product within a bigger market, e.g., those interested in mid-priced electric cars. Markets may be different types of interest or behaviour a brand might consider. For example, a hotel might look at the business traveller and the city break markets differently. Market can also be used to reflect a marketplace or platform through which brands are discovered and sold, e.g., concert tickets, travel or insurance.

MARKET OPPORTUNITY: A need or want in the market that is either unmet or under-served, presenting potential for growth.

MARKET SHARE: The percentage of total market sales that belongs to a brand or company.

MAXIMISE PROFIT: The process of increasing the difference between total revenue and total costs.

MESSAGING: How a brand communicates its value proposition to the target audience. Messaging must be consistent and authentic across audiences and products.

MUMSNET: A UK-based website/forum focused on parenting and family topics. It's become a platform for brand advertising and engagement.

MYSPACE: A social network popular in the early to mid-2000s, preceding Facebook.

NPS: Net Promoter Score. A popular customer satisfaction and loyalty metric used by businesses that asks how likely a customer is to recommend a business to a friend or family member, typically on a scale of 1–10.

OMNICHANNEL: A strategy integrating all communication channels so customers receive a joined-up experience across every touchpoint.

'OVER-ROTATED THE SHIFT TO DIGITAL': An example of a marketing-type jargon quote from former CEO of Nike, Mike Donohue, who has been criticised for weakening the Nike brand by focusing too much on spending in digital sales channels.

PAID RESPONSE ADVERTISING: Marketing designed to provoke immediate action from the audience, like buying or downloading something.

PC: Personal Computer. Prior to laptops, these were desktop devices typically used at home or work.

PEPSI TASTE CHALLENGE: A 1975 Pepsi campaign where consumers blindly taste-tested Pepsi vs Coke in malls, with consumers usually preferring Pepsi. These were converted into a TV campaign for Pepsi to try to switch Coca-Cola users to Pepsi.

PERCEPTUAL MAPS: Charts used to visually represent how consumers might perceive brands and products in comparison to those of competitors.

PERFORMANCE MARKETING vs BRAND MARKETING: This is among the biggest ongoing choices and debates in how to spend marketing funds. Performance marketing focuses spend on tactics, measurement and evaluation to deliver short-term sales. Brand marketing focuses more on spending to build brand awareness and differentiation, believing this pays back more in the longer term.

PIPELINE: A marketing or sales pipeline typically refers to the stages that a sales rep goes through to convert a lead into a customer. An email outreach campaign may identify prospects a salesperson might call, then try to book meetings with, then do proposals to, and then ultimately convert to a sale.

PPC: Pay-per-click. A digital advertising model in which advertisers pay only when a user clicks on their ad.

PR: Public Relations – the management of a brand's reputation and public perception through media and other non-paid promotional channels.

PRODUCT INNOVATION: The process of creating a new product or service – or improving an existing one – to meet customers' wants, desires and needs in a new way. Harvard Business School describes three types of innovation: sustaining innovation as the continuous improvement of an existing product; low-end disruption in which a company takes the bottom of the market by providing a 'good enough' product at a much lower cost; disruptive innovation where a company creates a new segment/product/service in a market that ultimately makes the incumbents obsolete.

PROFIT POTENTIAL: A projection of the highest achievable revenue after deducting all associated expenses.

PROTOTYPE: An early model used to test functionality, design or concept before a full-scale launch. Marketing campaigns or propositions may also be prototyped.

PURCHASE DECISION: The stage in the consumer decision-making process where an individual or organisation ultimately chooses whether or not to buy a product or service.

PURCHASE HISTORY: A record of a customer's past transactions with a business or retailer. It includes details such as the products purchased, dates, quantities, channel used, method of payment, delivery of product and prices.

QUALITATIVE vs QUANTITATIVE: Research that gathers in-depth, non-numeric insight (qualitative) vs measurable, statistically significant data (quantitative).

REAL-TIME MARKETING: Real-time marketing (RTM) leverages current information. It is the ability to adapt marketing to suit changes in a business's data or audience behaviour. RTM can also involve brands being topical and current in websites, customer service, ads, PR and social media.

REPOSITIONING: Changing how a brand/product is perceived by its target audience.

RETAINING DEMAND vs CREATING DEMAND: Demand is the number of your audience looking to buy your product or service. Creating demand is typically much harder in marketing as it means generating awareness and communicating a compelling value proposition and market positioning (so people choose your brand over competitors). To create demand by breaking into an established market or gaining market share can take considerable time and investment. Retaining demand, whilst not straightforward, should be easier to achieve. If the brand and its marketing have done their job properly, they should have built awareness, engagement and familiarity to encourage repeat purchases.

ROI: Return on investment. A metric used to measure the profitability of marketing efforts by comparing the revenue generated to the cost incurred.

SALESFORCE: A leading cloud-based CRM platform that helps businesses manage customer data, prospects and service.

SALES FUNNEL: A sales funnel, also sometimes called a purchase funnel. It is a visual and often numeric representation of the customer journey. It starts broad with the widest potential audience. It then represents different perceived stages as a customer goes from unaware to interested in buying (often described as a warm lead) to buying. The logic is that by plotting this journey a company can focus, evaluate and calculate the process and return of its marketing efforts at different stages to get an eventual sale.

SALES TARGET: The amount of products or services a company aims to sell within a given time period. These are often used to track performance and motivate sales teams.

SEARCH TERMS: Words or phrases typed into search engines. They indicate a user's intent and are monetised by platforms like Google for advertising where brands bid for what they see as the most important search terms.

SEO: Search engine optimisation. The process of optimising a website so search engines can better understand its content and help users find it via organic search (where search terms are not paid for but based on how a search engine ranks a website for factors such as audience, relevance or authority on a term).

SHOPIFY: A commerce platform that allows businesses to easily sell online, manage stores and scale operations.

SIDE-HUSTLE: An additional job or business outside someone's main job, sometimes started with the goal of becoming a full-time endeavour.

SILOED DEPARTMENTS: Functional divisions within organisations that operate in isolation, often hindering collaboration and integrated marketing. A company may separate sales, customer service, digital marketing, brand marketing, product development, etc. These also can have very separate and different evaluation objectives. A customer service department might be about how well it answers calls, yet a better answer for a customer might be to have no product issues in the first place or not have marketing expectations that the product fails on.

SOCIAL MEDIA: Websites, computer programs and platforms that allow people to communicate and connect by sharing information, opinions, pictures, videos, etc.

SOCIAL MEDIA INTERACTIONS: Any form of communication between a brand and social media users. It may be likes, comments, follows, tags, shares or even direct messages.

SPOTIFY: A digital service offering access to millions of songs, podcasts and videos. It has over 626 million monthly active users.

STORYTELLING: Using narrative in marketing to create emotional connection, build trust and improve brand memorability.

STRAPLINE: Also called a tagline, a short phrase that captures a brand's essence, e.g., Nike's 'Just do it'.

SUPPLY CHAIN: The network used in producing and delivering a product, from origin through to the final customer. As more and more businesses have outsourced aspects of their supply chain to reduce costs, this has sometimes caused major issues for brands to deliver on their promises when one link in the chain fails or increases in cost.

SUSTAINABLE FASHION: Clothing produced and consumed with minimised environmental and social impact across its entire lifecycle.

'THIS GIRL CAN' CAMPAIGN: A campaign that began in 2015 by Sport England encouraging women of all backgrounds and abilities to get active by trying to destigmatise how women felt when they tried to do sport and exercise.

TONE OF VOICE: The brand's communication style, affecting how its personality is perceived. It's about how something is said, not just what is said. Being 'authoritative' is very different to being 'humorous'.

TOUCHPOINTS: Any interaction between a customer and a brand, whether digital, physical or personal. A brand has multiple touchpoints. These include the physical such as in store or via a salesperson. They also include the virtual, such as a website.

TRADE STORY: The commercial rationale presented to distributors or third parties to encourage them to support a product or campaign.

TRUST: A fundamental foundation of strong customer relationships and loyalty in customers. In marketing, trust refers to a customer's belief in a company's or brand's ability and intention to deliver on its promises and provide value for what they desire, want or need.

UK CUSTOMER SATISFACTION INDEX: A benchmark of customer satisfaction in the UK, covering hundreds of organisations across sectors. UKCSI has been published twice a year since 2008. It measures on 278 organisations and organisation types in 13 sectors.

USER IP ADDRESSES: Unique identifiers assigned to internet-connected devices, enabling tracking, targeting, and message delivery.

UX: User experience. How a user interacts with a product, service, or system.

Companies aim to improve utility, ease of use and overall satisfaction. Companies don't just want a product, service or website. They ideally want one that delivers to expectations with minimal friction that could cause a customer to be frustrated or not complete their customer journey.

VISIBLE METRICS: Cause and effect in marketing are not always easily measurable. The effect of building a strong brand may generate returns over time but be harder to measure vs measuring click throughs from digital ads to a website. All aspects of the marketing mix will affect one another, e.g., price and place will affect sales and the effect of advertising response. Visible metrics refers to statistics that are easily observed and readily available in marketing. It is also a note of warning not to base marketing decisions and plans only on what is easily observed, as it may not reflect the true cause and effect.

VISUAL, SONIC OR BEHAVIOURAL IDENTITY: The broader sensory and behavioural elements representing a brand, such as sounds, colours, scents or tone.

WEBSITE (APP) BROWSING BEHAVIOUR: The pages customers or prospects have visited, the time they've spent on the site, and the number of times they've visited all provide insight into the effectiveness of what is being communicated and audience behaviour. Marketers can learn from this and change website design or communication to enhance the return they get when people land on their website.

WORDSMITH VALUES: When companies focus more on fancy language for their values than on whether the values are truly lived and reflected in actions.

ZEBRA STRIPING: An approach to parties and nights out where people alternate between drinking alcoholic and non-alcoholic drinks. This is to increase wellbeing and not feel so bad the next day. It is apparently popular with Gen Z.

Acknowledgements

To those who gave me a chance, inspired me or have been my thinking drinking buddies. Some are no longer with me. When I professionally studied marketing and research I read Dr Philip Kotler, but made home brew and laughed with Tim Orton. Tim went on to Specsavers and became my best man. The Tyneside Cinema gave me my first gig as a paid market researcher. I answered a small ad by John Duggan to get my first agency job. Rod Meadows patiently guided me on how to write a real strategic brief. Robin Wight and Stephen Woodford bet on me not to cock up the BMW brand at agency WCRS. There I met the best account man in the world, Stephen Knight (Tony Cadman, Peter Crossing, Steve Richards, Jorian Murray, Ed Will, Chris King, Will Harris, Michael Bray, Michael Moszynski . . . it was close). I was then offered what Sir Chris Powell described as a bigger canvas (more brands to work on and people to learn from) at BMP. There I met David Kean, the best new business director I've ever worked with. He's also my amazing editor on this book.

I've learned big strategic stuff working with the legends Peter Field and Les Binet. It's impossible to measure the benefits of countless interesting chats with my long-loose-list of strategic buddies. But it's creative people who stretched my thinking the most, the likes of Robin Wight, Larry and Rooney, Alan Jarvie, Dave Dye, Mark Fiddes, Martin Sharrocks, Andrew Cracknell, Don Barclay, Justin Shill and Kevin Mura. I was also told we'd once produced the worst ad ever seen by creative legend John Webster.

It's my special luck to be trusted to learn on great brand challenges with great clients, including: Simon Oldfield (BMW and Mercedes), David Wheldon OBE (Vodafone, Coca-Cola, Barclays and

Nat West), Simon Lowden and Neil Campbell (Pepsico), Mark Howe (Google), Lord MacLaurin and Terry Blake (English Cricket), Alan Dunachie and Andrew Rashbass (*The Economist*), Declan Moore (*National Geographic*), Ali Crossley (Legal & General), Kerin O'Connor and Julian Lloyd-Evans (Dennis), David Brook (Channel 4), Poppy Szkiler (Quiet Mark) and Miles Lewis and Spencer Hyman (LastFM).

Marc Lewis (the Dean of the School of Communication Arts), Claire Hewitt (Head of Learning Design at Henley Business School) and Donald Nekman (in association with Copenhagen Business School) persuaded me I should also teach.

I'd especially like to thank all those who still talk to me, or laugh with me, where I was once their boss (you know who you are). If I had a talent, it was finding them. Finally, I'd like to acknowledge that the best of the best leaders I ever worked with was Paul Taylor of BMP and OMD. He once introduced my role as lighting fires, and his role was sometimes fanning the flames and sometimes putting them out... and he meant it.

Index